Hispanic Devotional Piety

FAITH AND CULTURES SERIES

An Orbis Series on Contextualizing Gospel and Church
General Editor: Robert J. Schreiter, C.PP.S.

The *Faith and Cultures Series* deals with questions that arise as Christian faith attempts to respond to its new global reality. For centuries Christianity and the church were identified with European cultures. Although the roots of Christian tradition lie deep in Semitic cultures and Africa, and although Asian influences on it are well documented, that original diversity was widely forgotten as the church took shape in the West.

Today, as the churches of the Americas, Asia, and Africa take their place alongside older churches of Mediterranean and North Atlantic cultures, they claim their right to express Christian faith in their own idioms, thought patterns, and cultures. To provide a forum for better understanding this situation, the Orbis *Faith and Cultures Series* publishes books that illuminate the range of questions that arise from this global challenge.

Orbis and the *Faith and Cultures Series* General Editor invite the submission of manuscripts on relevant topics.

Also in the Series

Faces of Jesus in Africa, Robert J. Schreiter, C.PP.S., Editor

FAITH AND CULTURES SERIES

Hispanic Devotional Piety

Tracing the Biblical Roots

C. Gilbert Romero

ORBIS BOOKS

Maryknoll, New York 10545

The Catholic Foreign Mission Society of America (Maryknoll) recruits and trains people for overseas missionary service. Through Orbis Books, Maryknoll aims to foster the international dialogue that is essential to mission. The books published, however, reflect the opinions of their authors and are not meant to represent the official position of the society.

Copyright © 1991 by Orbis Books
All rights reserved
Published by Orbis Books, Maryknoll, New York 10545

Library of Congress Cataloging-in-Publication Data

Romero, C. Gilbert.
   Hispanic devotional piety : tracing the biblical roots / C.
Gilbert Romero.
     p. cm. — (Faith and cultures series)
   Includes bibliographical references and index.
   ISBN 0-88344-767-3
   1. Hispanic American Catholics—Religious life. 2. Catholics—
Latin America—Religious life. I. Title. II. Series.
BX1407.H55R66 1991
248′.089′68—dc20   91-18620
                                              CIP

Dedicated to
My Mother and Father

Contents

Acknowledgments   ix

Introduction   1

1. The Church and the Hispanic   5
   Partners or Adversaries?   5
   Church Response   7
   Latin American Bishops   10
   The Church in the United States   14

2. The Bible and Devotional Piety   15
   Heterogeneity of Hispanics   15
   The Term *Devotional Piety*   16
   Faith and Devotional Piety   17
   A Biblical Approach   19
   Insights from Cultural Anthropology   21
   Recent Biblical Hermeneutical Theory   27
   Four Devotions of Religiosidad Popular for Analysis   32

3. Revelation and Religiosidad Popular   34
   Church Teaching on Revelation   34
   Foundational and Dependent Revelation   37
   The Nature of Revelation   41
   The Function of Revelation   45
   Religiosidad Popular as Locus of Divine Revelation   47
   Summary and Conclusion   53

4. Ash Wednesday   57
   Explanation of the Devotion   57
   Biblical Analogues of Ashes   58
   Ashes in Religiosidad Popular Reflecting Analogues   63
   Insights from Anthropology and Hermeneutics   67
   Revelatory Aspect of Ash Wednesday   68
   Pastoral Implications   69

5. The Quinceañera   71
   Explanation of the Devotion   71

Biblical Analogues to the Quinceañera   73
Quinceañera in Religiosidad Popular Reflecting Analogues   78
Revelatory Aspect of the Quinceañera   80
Pastoral Implications   81

6. The Home Altar   **83**
Explanation of the Devotion   83
Biblical Analogues to the Home Altar   85
Political Implications of Tent and Ark Theologies   89
Home Altar in Religiosidad Popular Reflecting Analogues   91
Revelatory Aspect of the Home Altar   94
Pastoral Implications   96

7. The Penitentes   **98**
Explanation of the Devotion   98
Biblical Analogues to the Penitentes   101
Penitentes in Religiosidad Popular Reflecting Analogues   107
Revelatory Aspect of the Penitente Ritual   109
Pastoral Implications   111

8. Conclusions   **113**
Prospectus   113
Religiosidad Popular and Ecumenism   113
Religiosidad Popular and Liberation   116
Pastoral Orientation   119

Notes   **123**

Index   **137**

Acknowledgments

In a work that has spanned at least a decade, there are contributions from many sources too innumerable to acknowledge adequately. Those I single out are, first of all, the many academic and pastoral communities with which I have worked over the years and which have shared the wealth of their insights and experiences. Secondly, there is Archbishop Patricio Flores of San Antonio, Texas, whose courage and example of leadership and risk taking place him prominently among the select worthy successors of the apostles.

In addition, special thanks are due to those scholars who read and reacted to the first draft of the manuscript and made sound suggestions for improvement. They are: Rev. Avery Dulles, S.J., Rev. Gustavo Gutiérrez, Dr. Bernhard W. Anderson, Rev. Juan Romero, Sr. Nancy Wellmeier, S.N.D. de N., and Rev. Arturo Bañuelas. Distinct recognition must be given to Dr. Bernhard W. Anderson, who as a mentor taught me much about the Hebrew Scriptures, and to Rev. Avery Dulles, who has been most generous with his time and insight. A particular debt of gratitude is due to the team of pastoral agents who, during our monthly gatherings of 1977–78 in Albuquerque, New Mexico, helped me formulate the biblical and theological significance of Religiosidad Popular in a pastoral context. They were: Sr. Rosina Sandoval, SS.CC., Sr. Marie Luisa Vasquez, O.P., and Mrs. Albina Hernandez, all of Albuquerque, New Mexico; Sr. Eileen Hussey, O.P., of Estancia, New Mexico; and Sr. Nancy Wellmeier, S.N.D. de N., of Phoenix, Arizona.

Finally, no list of acknowledgments is complete without recognizing those whose vision and encouragement served as catalyst and impetus for me to begin and complete the project. Gustavo Gutiérrez and Enrique Dussel, who in private conversation first posed to me the challenge of a biblical analysis of Religiosidad Popular among U.S. Hispanics; Robert Ellsberg, editor in chief of Orbis, who saw possibility in the project; and William R. Burrows, also of Orbis, whose enduring patience kept me on track. To all of the above and those whose impact was felt on this work but not acknowledged, I am deeply grateful.

Introduction

My family has its cultural and religious roots firmly embedded in the enchanted soil of northern New Mexico. The "planting" of these paternal and maternal seeds goes back at least to the seventeenth century, a time soon after Juan de Oñate colonized the area in 1598. Every time that I visit relatives in northern New Mexico—Taos, Ranchos of Taos, Llano Quemado, Arroyo Hondo, Arroyo Seco, or Valdez—and participate in religious services, it is as if I am transported via a time warp back to a simpler age where the spirit was salutarily nourished through our old traditional cultural faith-expressions.

Our New Mexican faith-expressions were usually a combination of so-called official belief, expounded many years ago by a predominantly European clergy, and a sort of unofficial belief in God and in his workings in history. These unofficial faith-expressions were our devotions, made special because they were given expression in the idioms appropriate to our culture, namely local customs and the Spanish language.

As far back as I can remember, family devotions were the staple of religious identity, especially if they were devotions shared with the larger community. The classic example of this was the festal celebration of the town's patron saint, where there was an almost symbiotic relationship between religious and civic celebrations. For example, the fiestas of Santiago and Santa Ana (July 25, 26) in Taos; San Jeronimo (September 30) at the Taos pueblo, a couple of miles north of Taos, where the parish church was originally established; and the feast of Nuestra Señora del Carmen (July 16) in Llano Quemado. The usual triadic pattern of Mass, procession, and fiesta was common in these religious/civic fiestas.

But there were other devotional practices that helped constitute religious identity for our people. These devotional practices were generally keyed around the liturgical year, especially Christmas and Easter. Other significant devotional practices occurred around events meaningful in the lives of the people: rites of passage, feasts of the saints, pilgrimages, and the list could go on.[1] The important thing to recognize here is the significance of these and other devotional practices in the life and faith of the people, which were often more meaningful than official church worship.

It was this realization, coupled with personal experience of some of these devotional practices, that prompted me to investigate further the phenomenon of devotional piety among Hispanics, which is also called *religiosidad*

1

popular. * Religiosidad popular is a form of popular devotion among Hispanics, based more on indigenous cultural elements than on official Roman Catholic worship patterns. More will be said about this later. From childhood I can remember stories about Holy Week and the *Penitentes*; the day our family house was consecrated to the Sacred Heart; the daily family rosary; the seven-church pilgrimage on Holy Thursday; and other devotions. All these made an impression on me in my preteen years. These devotional practices and others like them were our anchors in a turbulent sea of cultural and ethnic pluralism.

Participation in a workshop on religiosidad popular in the summer of 1977 in Albuquerque, New Mexico,[2] led by Fr. Luis Maldonado from the *Instituto Superior de Pastoral* in Madrid, an extension of the University of Salamanca, Spain, functioned as the catalyst for my further investigations of the phenomenon of religiosidad popular as practiced among Hispanics in the Southwest. A team of six pastoral agents, including myself, gathered monthly for a year in the Albuquerque, New Mexico, area to study several significant devotional practices.[3] We each met with our respective target groups, most from around New Mexico, to hear what they had to say about their beliefs and devotional practices. Then we met to analyze and synthesize our insights. One of the concerns that kept surfacing repeatedly was the issue of relationship between the people's faith-expressions and their validity vis-à-vis the official church. Ultimately, the question was: Do these practices of devotional piety have a validity of their own as legitimate faith-expressions, or are they mere aberrations from what Catholic officialdom has called "normative" faith? Put into ecclesiastical terminology, the issue is whether or not this devotional piety could be validly considered as part of the authentic *sensus fidelium* so honored in church history.

Obviously the questions demanded an answer that took into account anthropological and theological issues that surfaced in the very asking of the question. Pastoral experience with Hispanics over the years, coupled with graduate study at Scripture at various institutions of higher learning, raised new questions for me and suggested possible avenues of exploration, especially through the Bible, since various parallels with certain practices of religiosidad popular began to suggest themselves. Time for serious reflection was provided during participation in an archaeological excavation at Tell-el-Hammah in the northern Jordan Valley of Palestine in the summer of 1988. There the quiet evenings after a hard day's work on the tell were as conducive of serious reflections as any library reading room. Refinement of some of the proposals set forth in this study occurred during the fall of 1989, during weekly pastoral visits and dialogue with the campesinos in the Santa Catalina Valley near the major seminary in Trujillo, Peru, where I

---

*A large number of Spanish words recur in this book. Italicizing them repeatedly would lead to a distracting text. Therefore we have decided generally to use regular type after introducing such words.

teach Scripture courses on a biennial basis. Though the Peruvian culture differs markedly from the Hispanic culture of the southwestern United States, enough parallel vestiges remain to show similarities in expressions of popular belief. The people's participation in the dialogue was most helpful.

The topic of religiosidad popular in the United States as a serious issue is of relatively recent interest to historians and social scientists, to say nothing of theologians or liturgists. Currently, the *Instituto de Liturgia Hispana*, a national organization of Hispanic liturgists, has been offering and continues to offer workshops nationally and locally on the different aspects of religiosidad popular. The most extensive of these workshops, as of this writing, was in Phoenix, Arizona, in October 1990, organized and coordinated by Fr. Juan Romero. The recently formed (1988) Academy of Catholic Hispanic Theologians in the United States has religiosidad popular as one of its principal areas of research.

One of the more insightful works on religiosidad popular and its pastoral approach in the United States was written by a Latin American theologian,[4] indicating a local paucity of solid theological material in the field. Is it only a Latin American theologian who can tell us something theologically and pastorally about our own Hispanic faith experiences here in the southwestern United States? A response in the negative was a partial catalyst for my writing this book. Others have dealt with religiosidad popular in Spain, Latin America, or the United States from a variety of perspectives.[5] Some works cited in the references of this book contain useful bibliographies in these areas. There is no attempt made here to provide an exhaustive bibliography on the topic of religiosidad popular. My aim is much more modest. What I purport to do is examine in depth a few significant practices of Hispanic devotional piety, taking into account insights from cultural anthropology and current biblical hermeneutical method as a way of understanding more clearly the phenomenon of religiosidad popular in the United States and its relationship to the Catholic church. While it is true that other cultures, Christian and non-Christian alike, experience rites of passage and penitential ceremonies, possess household shrines, and participate in other such rituals to express a communion with the divine, I shall deal only with the Hispanic cultural experience of devotional piety in the southwestern United States.

Chapter 1 sets the stage for understanding the relationship between the church and the Hispanic in the Southwest. From a historical perspective, easily the best current background work on the subject is the recent monograph by Moises Sandoval, *On the Move*.[6] The relational issue of the church and the Hispanic raises the question: Is the relationship between official church and the Hispanic friendly or adversarial? This is at the heart of the church's pastoral response to the reality of religiosidad popular. Chapter 2 focuses on the Bible and devotional piety, first by discussing the heterogeneity of U. S. Hispanics, clarifying the term *religiosidad popular* and the function of faith in religiosidad popular, then discussing what is meant by "Tracing the Biblical Roots" in the book's subtitle by providing the method that includes insights from cultural anthropology and recent biblical hermeneutical theory. Chapter 3 examines the theological notion of divine revelation as a key biblical category applicable to religiosidad popular. Chapters 4-7 examine specific devotional practices of religiosidad popular in light of the methodology described in chapter 2. Chapter 8 draws some conclusions, including a liberative dimension of religiosidad popular, and offers further suggestions for pastoral ministry. Because of this, I hope pastoral agents will profit from this investigation.

The central aim of this book is to show the theological legitimacy of Hispanic devotional piety as practiced in the southwestern United States, so that it can be truly appreciated from the "outside" and from "above" as both a theological locus and a basis for genuine spirituality. The Bible serves as the central point of discussion because of the pivotal role it plays in both Christian theology and Hispanic devotional piety.

I consider the connection between religiosidad popular and the Bible as very crucial, not only because of the latent richness in faith-expression made overt in active dialogue between the two, but also because of religiosidad popular's biblical grounding. I suspect that once Hispanic Catholics who are practitioners of religiosidad popular become aware of the biblical grounding of some of their devotions, they will be less likely to seek biblical affirmation of their beliefs elsewhere. This book attempts to ground religiosidad popular biblically.

Then there is the role of devotional practices in the general life of the Catholic church. For too long those devotional practices that didn't fit the official mold were called into question and, because of lack of cultural awareness, were sometimes vilified without any attempt at understanding, let alone appreciating. The church, as mother, has a responsibility to listen to the many voices of her children, which are often cries for understanding. I hope that this book will give words to the voice of religiosidad popular as it asks to be heard and understood. It asks to be heard and understood as a faith not limited by the strictures of Mediterranean culture, from whence it came, but as a faith beyond those boundaries, open and receptive to the experience of God in every cultural context.

1

The Church and the Hispanic

PARTNERS OR ADVERSARIES?

The relationship between the Catholic church and the Hispanic has been, and continues to be, complex. It is at times adversarial and at times benevolent. A cursory study of Latin American history from 1492 to the present will show that the church's failure to understand the faith and customs of indigenous peoples resulted in a neglect that had dire consequences, for example, by allowing social and religious control over the native peoples to fall into the hands of an avaricious state.[1] There were notable exceptions among some of the bishops during the early years of European colonization of Latin America, such as Bartolomé de las Casas of Chiapas, Mexico, and Antonio Validvieso of Nicaragua, who struggled on behalf of the native peoples by attempting to understand their culture and faith-expressions. Sadly, these bishops and others like them, even in modern times, were more the exception than the rule.

Admittedly, it is simplistic to attribute the adversarial relationship between church and the Latin American Indian solely to the church's failure to understand and encourage native culture and faith-expressions, but to minimize it as a major contributing cause would be equally simplistic and erroneous. Perhaps more than anything else, it was the exceedingly close relationship between the church and the governments of Spain and Portugal in the colonial period (sixteenth to eighteenth centuries) that resulted in mutually beneficial "special deals." An example of this was the state (Spain or Portugal) obtaining papal permission to control missionary lands and name their bishops in exchange for providing the church with special privileges.[2] This dubious liaison came to be known as "Cross and Crown" and "Christianity and Christendom." It came to exemplify the ultimate secular politicization of Christianity, making it virtually impossible for the church to exercise her prophetic function of challenging injustice wherever it might exist.

The 1987 film *The Mission* captured well the moral ambiguities of an excessively close church-state relationship in Latin America's colonial period, where the principal virtue of interaction was expediency rather than justice or compassion. The church's ill-fated attempt to pacify Spain and Portugal at the expense of sacrificing its missions resulted not only in the destruction of the missions but also in the church's loss of credibility among the Guarani Indians of Paraguay. The official church, represented by the cardinal in the film, promoted expediency. The Jesuits in the missions, in turn, were placed in a dilemma: either obey the official church authority and abandon the missions or obey the voice of conscience clamoring for sustained pastoral care toward the natives and face death. This was a classic conflict not totally unlike ones that exist today.

Throughout much of the colonial period there was the issue of devotional piety among the Latin American Indians as a defense against the Hispanicization of their native religion and culture. Enrique Dussel, a noted historian of Latin America, lists several positions adopted by the missionaries and Indians during the colonial era in Latin America with regard to Christianization.[3] Some evangelizers unconsciously mixed Hispanic (that is, Spanish) and Christian elements, as if they were identical, thereby confusing the natives into thinking that to be a good Christian meant to be a good Spaniard. In addition, many Indians were baptized without being thoroughly catechized, thus allowing for an amalgam of Christianity and native religious beliefs. Thus native devotional piety turned out to be both a bulwark against cultural imperialism and a concession to Christian evangelizing efforts. This volatile alliance between Christian dogma and native religion in the belief and worship of Latin American Indians has turned out to be a source of tension for the official church to the present day.[4]

In the United States there has been a similar history of neglect of the Hispanic by the church, quite likely, occasioned by the suspicions of a dominant Anglo-Irish (occasionally French) church toward any minority group that was considered nonconformist.[5] The nonconformity was felt most keenly in matters of belief and worship, where a strict orthodoxy and a stricter orthopraxis were normative for the local churches. There are many specific examples of church neglect of Hispanics in the United States.[6] In addition to the issue addressed in this book, two of the most common have been the delay or failure of some dioceses with large Hispanic populations to establish and promote diocesan-level ministries to Hispanics, and a seeming resistance to allow Sunday Masses to be celebrated in Spanish in parishes which have a sizable percentage of monolingual Hispanics.

One of the major problems facing the church today in her relationship with Hispanics is the fact that many Hispanics are turning to fundamentalist and evangelical churches and Pentecostal movements at an alarming rate. This phenomenon is surely indicative that something is wrong in the church-Hispanic relationship. Though various reasons are offered, it is safe to say that a major cause of this exodus has been the church's failure to recognize and accept the validity of Hispanic culture as a basic form of authentic religious expression.

CHURCH RESPONSE

Not all encounters between the church and the Hispanic have been negative, nor do I want to give that impression. In spite of a general history of practical church neglect of the Hispanic, the church has nonetheless expressed her concern primarily through public documentation.

Because devotional piety touches on liturgical expression, it was sometimes seen as rivaling the official liturgy, especially after the promotion of the Constitution on the Sacred Liturgy at the Second Vatican Council.[7] The constitution on the liturgy allowed for reform on several levels, perhaps the most profound being on the level of language. The vernacular could now be used in all forms of official worship. Latin, which very few others outside the Vatican understood, was no longer the only language of worship. Luis Maldonado points out that language, when used in devotional piety, is spoken in biblical form, that is, symbolic as narrative, poetic, sapiential.[8] Yet it is not the speaking as such that characterizes the practitioner of devotional piety, but the symbolic action, the ritual. In other words, devotional piety as worship is more expressive of the five senses working in tandem than abstract thought or the recitation of formulaic prayers.[9]

One of the major sources of tension between the official church and devotional piety has been the official (Latin-Western) church's tendency toward centralization of authority and push toward conformity. Maldonado suggests that by contrast the oriental (non-Latin) churches have always maintained the importance of the local church, thus affirming the local culture together with its language and customs. This sensitivity to the people subsequently resulted in a kind of cultural pluralism expressed in different liturgical families—Byzantine, Coptic, Maronite, Armenian, to name a few. On the other hand, in the Latin church the Holy See, as the sole legislator in such cases, has promoted liturgical conformity and centralization of authority. This uniformity, rather than uniting the diverse peoples, only fragmented them from official worship because the language and cultural expression of official worship were alien to them.[10] At the same time, we must express a caution regarding the risk of assuming automatically that cultural pluralism brings about unity. The potential for divisiveness is always present in the tendency toward preservation of national customs and language. Our history in the United States with regard to national parishes has taught us that. The cultural sword is double-edged; it cuts in favor of unity as well as of divisiveness. Avery Dulles says that ". . . cultural pluralism where it exists, calls for strong structures and symbols of unity to prevent it from becoming divisive."[11] Church documentation that focuses on culture and devotional piety helps to provide those strong structures and symbols of unity.

The first modern document to provide perspective on devotional piety within the context of official church worship may be said to be the Vatican II document *Sacrosanctum Concilium*, the Constitution on the Liturgy, promulgated on December 4, 1963.

Even in the liturgy the Church does not wish to impose a rigid uniformity in matters which do not involve faith or the good of the whole community. Rather does she respect and foster the qualities and talents of the various races and nations. Anything in these people's way of life which is not indissolubly bound up with superstition and error she studies with sympathy, and, if possible, preserves intact. She sometimes even admits such things into the liturgy itself, provided they harmonize with its true and authentic spirit (37).[12]

A second document of note is the encyclical *Evangelii Nuntiandi* of Pope Paul VI, December 8, 1975.[13] In this encyclical Pope Paul sees evangelization as a process of total interior transformation, not only of individuals but of societies as well. It goes on to say that the transformation is at the "... very centre and roots of life. The gospel must impregnate the culture and the whole way of life of man ..." (20). The Gospel and evangelization penetrate all cultures while subservient to none. The message of evangelization is to relate to human life on social as well as personal levels. "It must deal with community life in society, with the life of all nations, with peace, justice, and progress. It must deliver a message, especially relevant and important in our age, about liberation" (29). This form of liberation seeks to establish justice in charity (35).

The primary means for this liberative evangelization are personal example, preaching, and catechetical instruction (41-47). In addition to these three there is a fourth that merits serious consideration, and Paul VI calls this means popular religiosity, which ...

if it is prudently directed and especially when it is directed along the path and according to the methods of evangelization, it may be productive of great good. For it does indicate a certain thirst for God such as only those who are simple and poor in spirit can experience. It can arouse in men capacity for self-dedication and for the exercise of heroism when there is a question of professing the faith. It gives man a keen sensitivity by virtue of which he can appreciate the ineffable attributes of God: his fatherly compassion, his providence, his benevolence and loving presence. It can develop in the inmost depths of man habits of virtue rarely to be found otherwise in the same degree, such as patience, acceptance of the Cross in daily life, detachment, openness to other men and a spirit of ready service. It is on account of these qualities that we prefer to call it *popular piety* or the religion of the people rather than *religiosity* ... Above all, we must be sympathetic in our approach, quick to appreciate its inherent nature and its desirable qualities and zealous to direct it so that the dangers arising out of its errors may be avoided. When it is wisely directed, popular piety of this kind can make a constantly increasing contribution toward bringing the masses of our people into contact with God in Jesus Christ (48).[14]

Paul VI sees devotional piety in very positive terms, especially as an effective tool for evangelization. Among the many notable comments in the lengthy citation is the strong affirmation of the cultural values in devotional piety for developing a genuine spirituality: compassion, sensitivity, awareness of God, patience, and other virtues that seem to flourish more easily in a context of popular religiosity, quite likely because the life-style of practitioners of popular religiosity tends toward the simple and uncomplicated, and thus has greater openness to transcendence.

Quite possibly, one of the most revolutionary documents to issue forth from the Second Vatican Council is *Gaudium et Spes*, the Pastoral Constitution on the Church in the Modern World, issued December 7, 1965. The revolutionary aspect of this document is measured more in terms of what it implies rather than what it states. The preface and introduction speak directly to the hopes and aspirations of humanity with suggestions for improving the social order. With regard to religion, the document makes incisive observations.

As regards religion there is a completely new atmosphere that conditions its practice. On the one hand people are taking a hard look at all magical world-views and prevailing superstitions and demanding a more personal and active commitment of faith, so that not a few have achieved a lively sense of the divine. On the other hand greater numbers are falling away from the practice of religion (7).[15]

This new atmosphere regarding the practice of religion to which the document refers is predicated on the seismic shifts in values taking place on a world scale. At the time of the Second Vatican Council there were ongoing movements such as growth of the military-industrial complex, expansion of multinational corporations, quantum-leap advancements in technology, spread of the counterculture, and a wide diffusion of consumerism. Mainstream Christianity, as a repository of traditional values such as compassion, justice, care for the poor, and so forth, was threatened if not already in decline. *Gaudium et Spes* was refocusing human energy to center on human dignity, and religion was to be the key (11, 25).

In the pastoral methodology provided by the document significant attention is paid to the proper development of culture (53–62).

It is one of the properties of the human person that he can achieve true and full humanity only by means of culture, that is through the cultivation of the goods and values of nature. Whenever, therefore, there is a question of human life, nature and culture are intimately linked together.

The word "culture" in the general sense refers to all those things which go to the refining and developing of man's diverse mental and physical endowments ... Hence it follows that culture necessarily has historical and social overtones, and the word "culture" often carries with it sociological and ethnological connotations; in this sense one can speak about a plurality of cultures. For different styles of living and different scales of values originate in different ways of using things, of working and self-expression, of practicing religion and of behavior, of developing science and the arts and of cultivating beauty (53).

Culture thus plays an important role in human development, especially through the linkage it provides with religion, and in particular, faith (57). The various expressions of faith provided by different cultures are to be recognized and encouraged, but with the usual caveats (58).

Finally, the document recognizes the tension that has existed and continues to exist between the official church and various cultures in its attempt to harmonize the various cultures with Christian thought. Thus theologians are given the specific task of bridging the gap as best as possible while maintaining the integrity of both the church and the different cultures (62). And from what has been said above, we can conclude the document's implicit endorsement of valid cultural expressions of religious belief, such as devotional piety.

LATIN AMERICAN BISHOPS

The Latin American bishops' conference of 1968 in Medellín, Colombia, while indirectly endorsing the movement known as liberation theology in the political sphere, also underscored the need to recognize the cultural and religious transformation taking place on the continent. Evangelization in Latin America was undergoing difficulties due to demographic expansionism, socio-cultural changes, personnel shortages of evangelizers, and other similar causes. Evangelization, as focused primarily through the sacraments, was more successful insofar as it availed itself of social structures such as family and church community. It was because of the use of social structures such as these that evangelization in Latin America prospered. These social structures of family and church community are natural resources for the evangelization potential of religiosidad popular.

Document number 6 of Medellín on *Pastoral Popular*[16] spoke about evangelization through devotional piety. The document recognizes the need for the Latin American to express his or her faith in a simple, emotional, and collective manner—methods conducive to devotional piety. Faith comes wrapped in a cultural language, and in proclaiming her faith, the church must be open to the different cultural expressions of that faith.

There are theological principles (5-9) and pastoral recommendations (10-15) that Medellín offers with regard to devotional piety. With regard to theological criteria, there is first the church's attempt to discover God's presence in devotional piety, which is culturally diversified, and to accept, purify, and incorporate into the order of faith the different religious and human elements in devotional piety that can be considered a *preparatio evangelica*, that is, a basis for promoting church teaching (section 5).

Secondly, people cling to the faith and participate in the church on different levels. On the one hand it should not be presupposed that there is an act of faith behind every religious expression that is apparently Christian. Nor should we arbitrarily deny the true faith-character of any faith-expression that we don't understand or whose motivation we find suspect. True faith seeks to authenticate itself.

Finally, faith authentication will come about through a reevangelization and reconversion process elaborated through a pastoral plan emphasizing not only the personal but also (and more importantly) the social dimensions of faith.

The document then offers very practical pastoral recommendations for the Latin American continent that touch directly on devotional piety. Among some of the more salient are: a serious and systematic study of devotional piety; realization of a liturgico-catechetical pastoral plan for all people, not just small groups; revision of devotion to saints to include viewing saints as role models, not just as intercessors; formation of ecclesial communities in the parish centered around family, and that these communities maintain strong connections with Scripture, sacrament, and the bishop's authority.

A second document of major importance to come from the Latin American bishops in their consideration of devotional piety is the final declaration of the third CELAM (Latin American bishops' conference) meeting in Puebla, Mexico, 1979.[17] A major concern at Puebla, as at Medellín, was an adequate evangelization of the Latin American continent. Several means are suggested, and one of the most promising is that of devotional piety.

Picking up on Paul VI's *Evangelii Nuntiandi*, the document shares his definition of and concerns for culture, and reemphasizes the need to evangelize it. The task of the evangelization of culture is ". . . to get at the very core of a culture, the realm of its basic values, and to bring about a conversion that will serve as the basis and guarantee of a transformation in structures and the social milieu" (338). True evangelization takes the whole human being into account, and this means the culture in which a person's values find configuration, namely language and customs. The church does what it can to adapt itself (404).

Language and customs as cultural constitutives find their religious expression in devotional piety. Puebla strongly affirms this in its definition of devotional piety, though Puebla, as did Paul VI, refers to this phenom-enon as "popular piety."[18]

> By the religion of the people, popular religiosity or popular piety, we
> mean the whole complex of underlying beliefs rooted in God, the
> basic attitudes that flow from these beliefs, and the expressions that
> manifest them. It is the form of cultural life that religion takes on
> among a given people. In its most characteristic cultural form, the
> religion of the Latin American people is an expression of the Catholic
> faith. It is a people's Catholicism (444).

As part of the affirmation of devotional piety, the document goes on to state the great values that this piety offers in dealing with the great ques-tions of life, providing a common wisdom that is ". . . capable of fashioning a vital synthesis." Furthermore, devotional piety

> . . . creatively combines the divine and the human, Christ and Mary,
> spirit and body, communion and institution, person and community,
> faith and homeland, intelligence and emotion. This wisdom is a Chris-
> tian humanism that radically affirms the dignity of every person as a
> child of God, establishes a basic fraternity, teaches people how to
> encounter nature and understand work, and provides reasons for joy
> and humor in the midst of a very hard life. For the common people
> this wisdom is a principle of discernment and an evangelical instinct
> through which they spontaneously sense when the Gospel is served
> in the Church, and when it is emptied of its content and stifled by
> other interests (448).
> Because this cultural reality takes in a very broad range of social
> strata, the common people's religion is capable of bringing together
> multitudes. Thus it is in the realm of popular piety that the Church
> fulfills its imperative of universality . . . (449).

The transformative and social dimension of devotional piety is under-scored in the document by attributing to it a liberative dimension, namely, the awareness of needs within the normal groupings, for example, neigh-borhood and village, and the resolution to deal with those needs in a con-crete way (452). So that devotional piety not be idealized to the point of accepting it uncritically, the document presents some of its negative aspects. Indeed, there are certain positive elements in devotional piety that should be affirmed. In addition to what was mentioned above (448), there are the following qualities:

> . . . the trinitarian presence evident in devotions and iconography; a
> sense of God the father's providence; Christ celebrated in the mystery
> of his Incarnation (the Nativity, the child Jesus), in his crucifixion, in

the Eucharist, and in the devotion to the Sacred Heart. Love for Mary is shown in many ways ... Other positive features are: veneration of the saints as protectors; remembrance of the dead; an awareness of personal dignity and of solidary brotherhood; awareness of sin and of the need to expiate it; the ability to express the faith in a total idiom that goes beyond all sorts of rationalism (chant, images, gesture, color, and dance); faith situated in time (feasts) and in various places (sanctuaries and shrines); a feel for pilgrimage as a symbol of human and Christian existence; filial respect for their pastors as representatives of God; an ability to celebrate the faith in expressive and communitarian forms; the deep integration of the sacraments and sacramentals into their personal and social life; a warm affection for the person of the Holy Father; a capacity for suffering and heroism in withstanding trials and professing their faith; a sense of the value of prayer; and acceptance of other people (454).

Nevertheless, there are negative aspects to devotional piety that must be considered. These negative elements usually occur when the official church is not actively involved in dialoguing with devotional piety. Examples of some negative aspects of devotional piety are: superstition, fatalism, static archaism, misinformation and ignorance, syncretistic reinterpretation, reduction of faith to mere contact with God, secularism, sectarianism, manipulation of various types, to name some (456).

The presence of these negative elements in devotional piety underscores the need for evangelizing by entering into serious dialogue with devotional piety. A type of pastoral pedagogy is needed, with perhaps the most important ingredient being knowledge of "... the symbols, the silent nonverbal language of the people. Only then can we engage in a vital dialogue with them, communicating the Good News through a renewed process of informational catechesis" (457).[19] Such a pedagogy of evangelization, to be effective in Latin America, demands that the agents of evangelization ". . . love the people and be close to them"; that the purpose of the pedagogy is to make the people "more truly the children of God" (458–459).

Certainly no other major church document has so thoroughly examined and subsequently endorsed the value of devotional piety as that from Puebla. Even with the recognition of the problem of potential abuse in devotional piety, Puebla attests to the inherent values in devotional piety and seeks to promote them not only for the evangelization of the Latin American peoples, but also for their spirituality and liberative aspect as well. What has been said in the Puebla document concerning devotional piety in the context of Latin America may also be said of devotional piety among Hispanics of the southwestern United States, since there is a distinct parallelism and strong linkage between the two.[20]

THE CHURCH IN THE UNITED STATES

The response of the Catholic bishops of the United States to the pastoral needs of Hispanics took form primarily in documentation and support of various programs. Perhaps the most significant document to come forth from the U.S. bishops regarding Hispanics is the *National Plan for Hispanic Ministry*,[21] which was the outcome of the *Tercer Encuentro Nacional Hispano de Pastoral*,[22] which itself was convoked officially by the bishops in their 1983 pastoral letter, *Hispanic Presence: Challenge and Commitment*.[23]

The National Pastoral Plan places the framework of Hispanic reality, among other things, in the context of culture, offering virtually the same assessment as *Evangelii Nuntiandi* and the Puebla document.

> Some values that make up the Hispanic culture are a "profound respect for the dignity of each person ... deep and reverential love for family life ... a marvellous sense of community ... a loving appreciation for God's gift of life ... and an authentic and consistent devotion to Mary ..." Culture for Hispanic Catholics has become a way of living out and transmitting their faith. Many local practices of popular religiosity have become widely accepted cultural expressions. Yet the Hispanic culture, like any other, must continue to be evangelized.[24]

The bishops' pastoral letter, in order to understand Hispanic culture, proposes further investigation of the ties United States' Hispanics have with Latin America.[25] This investigation will lead to a deeper understanding of United States' Hispanic spirituality, of which various nontraditional prayer forms and traditions have been characteristic. The values inherent in these prayer forms must be investigated and studied thoroughly in order for there to be a true appreciation of United States' Hispanic spirituality. Again, the bishops reinforce Paul VI's affirmation of devotional piety. But certainly, the most trenchant observation from a pastoral point of view is that ...

> A closer dialogue is needed between popular and official practice, lest the former lose the guidance of the Gospel and the latter lose the active participation of the unsophisticated and the poorest among the faithful. An ecclesial life vibrant with a profound sense of the transcendent such as is found in Hispanic popular Catholicism, can also be a remarkable witness to the more secularized members of our society.[26]

It is with this in mind—the need for dialogue between Hispanic devotional piety and the official church, which has shown support of and continued concern for a better understanding of devotional piety—that this present study is undertaken.

2

The Bible and Devotional Piety

The church documents mentioned in the preceding chapter have left no doubt that the official church sees great value in devotional piety and strongly encourages its study for understanding. In this chapter we shall explore ways to better understand Hispanic devotional piety, with special emphasis on the role of the Bible. But first a clarification of terms.

HETEROGENEITY OF HISPANICS

When we speak of Hispanics in the United States, we could be speaking of any one of a multiethnic, heterogeneous group with roots in South America, Central America, the Caribbean, Puerto Rico, or Mexico. It is difficult, if not impossible, to choose a universally acceptable nomenclature, because the differences among the various groups are so pronounced. The predominant basis of identity among these groups varies with context and motive. For example, the basis could be political (as with the term Chicano), social, ethnic, geographic, or any one of several other possibilities. For purposes of this investigation, I will employ what is generally considered the least-problematic term: Hispanics. The specific referents for this study of devotional piety will be primarily, though not exclusively, the Mexican Americans of the southwestern United States, where the proximate cultural and religious roots are in Mexico. The reason for this is principally pragmatic. They are the most dominant Hispanic group in the United States, and I have more familiarity with them in pastoral contexts.[1]

However, it is necessary to point out that in addition to Mexican roots, the phenomenon of Hispanic devotional piety in the southwestern United States owes much to Latin American sources as well. Also, because of the colonial experience in sixteenth-century Latin America, there are vestiges of Spanish influence in Latin American faith-expressions. As immigrants from Mexico and South America evangelized principally by Spaniards, these Hispanics come to the United States with their faith-traditions. In order to comprehend the origins of their faith-traditions, we find ourselves.

much like archaeologists who examine a mound stratigraphically, pushing back the surface evidence layer by layer. In order to understand Hispanic devotional piety in the United States, it is also necessary, as the American bishops say in their pastoral letter, to investigate ties with Latin America. Thus in the course of our discussion both Mexican and Latin American theologians will be cited as they themselves attempt to come to grips with the theological understanding of devotional piety in their own proper contexts.[2]

THE TERM *DEVOTIONAL PIETY*

Like the Hispanics themselves, their faith-expressions are known by different names, though the dynamics of belief are virtually the same. Paul VI went to great lengths to be precise in his understanding of the phenomenon he called popular piety (*Evangelii Nuntiandi* 48). He called it popular because it was a religion of the people, and he called it piety as opposed to the formalities of religiosity, which he distinguishes. For Paul VI, the word *piety* conveys, in a way formal religiosity does not, that thirst for God which only the simple and "poor in spirit" can experience. That simple faith also gives a certain sensitivity to appreciate God's compassion, benevolence, and presence. Furthermore, this piety develops those virtues that are most truly experienced in adversity.

Puebla, in its attempt to clarify its usage of the phrase, winds up making three terms interchangeable: *religiosidad popular, piedad popular*, and *Catolicismo popular* (444). Basically, as Puebla explains, this popular piety is the complex of deeply rooted religious beliefs of the people in God, and those attitudes and expressions that flow from those religious beliefs. It is, as Puebla consistently emphasizes, the simple faith of the Latin American people — a people's Catholicism as opposed to the more formally structured hierarchical Catholicism.

Though Medellín titles its document on popular piety *Pastoral Popular*, indicating the evangelizing focus of popular devotions, the term commonly used throughout the document is "religiosidad popular," a term and its explanation that Puebla accepts and expands in its discussion of popular piety. Because Medellín was the first major document on the subject of popular piety by the Latin American bishops,[3] the term religiosidad popular became canonized and was the most common way of expressing the concept of popular piety in Spanish.[4]

This usage of terminology is not a hollow exercise in semantics. Far from it. Rather, as Paul VI took great pains to be precise in his choice of terminology because he felt that use of the proper term conveyed a deeper and more veritable meaning behind the reality, so I feel it necessary to explain my use of the term devotional piety in the remainder of the work, in order to avoid misunderstanding. I accept the canonical usage of the term religiosidad popular, but my translation for it is devotional piety. First of all, the word *piety* for me conveys the notion of the deep faith of simple people (simple in the sense of the Spanish word *sencillo*, unpretentious) and all of the positive values profferred by Paul VI and Puebla. The adjectival designate *devotional* best describes the concrete, indigenous, cultural expressions of this deep and simple faith. Hence my choice of the term.

FAITH AND DEVOTIONAL PIETY

In the Hispanic southwestern United States, there is a large number of people of Mexican descent with growing numbers from South and Central America.[5] So it is both difficult and unreal to rigidly delimit one group over against another regarding religious beliefs. It would be safe to say that in the course of this study, the dynamics of faith with regard to religiosidad popular are virtually the same for Mexican Americans and Latin Americans in the southwest. Even some devotional practices, such as Marian devotions, pilgrimages, and celebration of meaningful moments in the life cycle, are common to both groups, so that while we can speak of differences, we can also speak of similarities in our analysis. It has been my experience that interaction between the Mexican Americans and Latin Americans in the southwestern faith-communities has permitted a kind of symbiosis vis-à-vis religiosidad popular. One of these similarities is the nature of faith itself.

The experiences of multilevel oppression and its attendant suffering are common in the history of Mexico[6] and Latin America.[7] This experience, coupled with the feeling of political powerlessness in dealing with the oppressor, allowed the Hispanic—Mexican American and Latin American—to respond in the only way effectively possible, through simple expressions of that faith or devotional piety. When these people emigrated to the southwestern United States, oppression on a somewhat modified scale continued to be their lot in life. Thus their faith and devotional piety became their means of self-assertion.

A parallel can be made between Hispanic devotional piety and the years of early Christianity, when the rise of apocalyptic literature offered similar solace and hope to a people experiencing anxiety, a sense of powerlessness, and exploitation (ca. 200 B.C.E. to ca. 200 C.E.). In this type of context, imagery and symbolism from Scripture take on an added dimension of meaning when filtered through a people's experience of adversity. The apocalyptic movement of the early church could well have been a prototype for Hispanic devotional piety, in the sense that in both cases there was an appropriation of Scripture via culturally conditioned imagery and symbolism interpreted in a given historical context that spoke meaningfully to specific situations of anxiety, feelings of powerlessness, and exploitation.

The faith expressed in Hispanic devotional piety may be likened to that experience of transcendence described by Rudolf Otto as "numinous experience," the idea of the holy. One Mexican theologian speaks of devotional piety as having a "substratum of faith"; that is, consisting of an alpha and omega, the ambiguities and impurities of faith hovering around the alpha, while the mature and liberative elements surround the omega part of the spectrum.[8] As rural inhabitant, the Mexican peasant is in touch with nature, and in an attempt to understand the forces of nature operating in daily life, he generally hovers around the alpha stage of religious faith. In order to understand the transcendental element in the alpha range of religiosidad popular, with hope of nudging it toward the omega side, it is first necessary to appreciate the world of myth and symbolism as response to that experience of transcendence.[9] Myth can be seen as the aesthetic intellectual expression of religiosidad popular,[10] for in myth there is usually encountered the conflict between good and evil, often personified. Myths can become legends if their heroes embody the specific victory over evil and chaos that the particular myth proposes. Since conflict is very much a part of daily life, there is almost always an attempt to understand its origin and meaning in order to deal with it. Devotion to the saints may well run the risk of this legendary treatment with mythic overtones in the attempt to understand the nature of and victory over conflict.

However, the correct approach to the relationship between faith and devotional piety is a critical one. One must both evaluate the ambiguities of religiosidad popular and assess its positive aspects.[11] Given the Christological focus of our Christian faith to which religiosidad popular responds, Ernest Henan's positive assessment of that popular faith states:

> Neither our confession of Jesus as God-with-us nor our readiness to walk in his footsteps originates, however, in a personal encounter with the man Jesus. We only know him from a tradition in which he is expressed. He is mediated to us from a linguistic tradition and an extended world of images. Popular religion is one of the ways in which this world of symbols is transmitted and it constitutes the expression of our consent to the reality to which that language and those symbols point. Both the case for popular religiosity and the relative value of its legitimacy originate on the one hand in the tension that is always present in language, symbols and modes of expression and, on the other, in the reality to which those factors refer.[12]

This tension is alleviated to the extent that the faith of the believer is in tune with normative Catholic doctrine. It is the function of those responsible for this normative Catholic doctrine to promote a critical perspective of devotional piety. Segundo Galilea provides some insights into faith as a critical perspective on religiosidad popular, and though he speaks about the situation in Latin America, there are distinct parallels with conditions in the southwestern United States.[13]

Given the fact that much of religiosidad popular in Latin America is a combination of sixteenth-century Iberian Christianity and pre-Columbian religion, the resultant faith-expressions are, according to Galilea, in a state of decadence that has resulted in a sort of "de-Christianization" of normative belief. Reasons for this are basically economic, historical, and sociopolitical. Religiosidad popular is a Christian faith born out of a context of oppression and marginality. It is a faith that rationalizes its oppression and seeks compensation for its social frustrations, often lending itself to manipulation. In Latin America, religiosidad popular is a religion of the poor who have experienced a poverty generated primarily by injustice, which colors its often negative view of society and the world. There is frequently the danger of "secularization," namely the domination of nature by technology, thus demythifying religious myths and replacing them with secular ones, such as the omnipotence of technology in the United States and of the state in Latin America. This view of life and society is in need of evangelization or, more accurately, the critical perspective of "faith."

By faith as critical principle, Galilea means the Gospel of Jesus Christ (an abbreviation for normative Catholic beliefs). The first level of critique with respect to religiosidad popular is to develop a historical sense that is latent in the Gospel message, that is to say that faith is not merely a personal affair but more importantly a community experience. The believing community remembers the "saving acts of God," such as its own Exodus journey through the wilderness to a promised land, deliverance from all enemies, and affirmation of its messianic hopes. It is only with this sense of a historical dimension that religiosidad popular can be affirmative and pass on to the omega point of faith.

The second level of faith as critique is the promotion of the Gospel message (which is latent in religiosidad popular) as the paradigm for society. This would mean giving one, especially the poor, a sense of human dignity by proclaiming justice and inviting the other to belong to the "kingdom of God." When Jesus invited people to enter into his Kingdom, there were sociopolitical consequences. The critical dimension of Gospel faith directed toward religiosidad popular makes the same invitation with equally expectant results.[14]

A BIBLICAL APPROACH

The heart of any understanding of religiosidad popular lies in establishing its relationship with the Bible as a primary source of symbolism and imagery. The question of relating religiosidad popular to the Bible is the age-old problem of relating an ancient text written in a different language within a different culture to a contemporary situation. This is the challenge, to adapt Gadamer's term, of "fusing the two horizons," that of the past's meaning with that of the present. This dual hermeneutical posture of "What did the biblical text mean then?" and "What does the biblical text mean now?" has kept biblical scholars busy for at least three decades, searching for ways to fuse the horizons with integrity. The development of literary theory and the utilization of social sciences have broadened the scope of biblical study and enabled scholars to bring about the fusion more easily.

Apart from understanding the nature of the relationship between the Bible and religiosidad popular, there is first the question of the relationship itself. Why is the Bible important to Hispanic devotional piety? First of all, we must recognize an already existing bond between the two, in that Hispanics feel a strong attraction to the word of God as expression of ongoing dialogue. I suspect that people who have experienced poverty and struggle and can find parallels to their own lives in a sacred literature will be drawn to that sacred literature as a source of comfort and hope. This is one of the reasons why the Old Testament, or more correctly the Hebrew Scriptures known as TANAK,[15] has been such a rich resource for Latin American liberation theology and can be such for religiosidad popular. TANAK* offers more concrete examples than the Christian Scriptures for varied communal experiences of God's love, mercy, compassion, and forgiveness in a context of struggle for maturation.

A more concrete connection between the Bible and religiosidad popular is suggested by Mexican theologian Raul Vidales. He says that Mexicans have a religious age equal to that of the Old Testament; that is, the age of Abraham and Israel. By that he means that Abraham and Israel, in their search for deepening their relationship with Yahweh, were bound to a culture, a rudimentary language, and an incipient ritualistic and symbolic world. In effect, ". . . the religious practice of our [Mexican] people is characterized by Old Testament traits."[16] This is especially evident in the use of symbols and language that are indigenous and rise from the experience of the people. Another perception of the relationship between religiosidad popular and the Old Testament is that offered by Herman Vorländer, who sees religiosidad popular in the Old Testament as popular perception of God's direct involvement in lives of the individual, community, and nature, apart from official religion.[17]

Secondly, one can note a strong messianic focus in both TANAK and religiosidad popular, as well as a predisposition for anthropomorphism and personification. Indeed, both are symbol rich. And it is primarily for these reasons that in my biblical analysis I will be utilizing TANAK in relationship to religiosidad popular. Thirdly—and this is the basic pastoral reason—the Bible can help mediate an effective dialogue between the institutional church and religiosidad popular, thus providing an excellent tool for evangelization as asked for in particular by Paul VI and Puebla.

What do I mean by "a biblical approach" to Hispanic devotional piety? First of all, I recognize an already existing relationship between the Bible and Hispanic devotional piety, in that the former is a fundamental spiritual resource for the latter, and I will attempt to explore the nature of that

*See note 15. We shall use the acronym "TANAK" throughout this book instead of the term "Old Testament."

relationship. Secondly, as part of that exploration I will utilize a methodology that takes into account the insights of language theory insofar as it touches upon the interpretation of the biblical text, the insights of cultural anthropology as one of the useful social sciences, and recent developments in biblical hermeneutical theory—insofar as these touch upon a better understanding of Hispanic devotional piety. The ultimate aim will be to facilitate the process of evangelization. Since I accept the existing relationship between the Bible and Hispanic devotional piety as a given and will postpone the insights of language theory until later, I will continue with a discussion of the insights of cultural anthropology and recent discussion in biblical hermeneutical theory.

INSIGHTS FROM CULTURAL ANTHROPOLOGY

The social sciences have played a significant role recently in biblical interpretation. Chief among these has been sociology.[18] Gaining in importance, at least as far as biblical research is concerned, is anthropology, more specifically cultural anthropology, which is the social science most suitable for giving us a "secular" and "scientific" understanding of religiosidad popular. For religiosidad popular culture and faith are at the root of its identity. What we would call culture in this context would be the Hispanic people's language, customs, imagery, symbolism, worldviews, and the faith-expressions through which these are made manifest. Thus Hispanic culture at the base of religiosidad popular can be viewed as a creative force enabling the practitioners to be subjects and not objects of their history, as often happens when non-Hispanics define Hispanic realities.

Terminology within any given discipline, though somewhat arbitrary and ambiguous, nevertheless serves a useful purpose in delimiting discussion. Such is the case with the term *supracultural*. As Charles Kraft observes:

The adjective "supracultural," however, serves a very useful purpose in signifying the transcendence of God with respect to culture. That is, God, being completely unbound by any culture (except as he chooses to operate within or in terms of culture) is *supra*cultural (i.e. above and outside culture). Likewise, any absolute principles or functions proceeding from God's nature, attributes, or activities may be labeled "supracultural." For they, too, transcend and are not bound by any specific culture, except when they are expressed within a culture.[19]

God as supracultural is perceived and personalized in relationship to a given culture, specifically within the context of prayer and worship. In the case of Hispanics of the southwestern United States, this personalized relationship with a supracultural God takes place within the framework of their devotional piety.

Since the relational aspect of God occurs within the context of a given culture, that relation is relativized by those outside the culture; for example, Europeans thinking that Hispanic practices are "quaint." This stance of cultural relativism toward God provides for an understanding of one ethnic group's perception of God by another, but at the same time there needs to be a caution against what, in an oxymoronic sense, can be termed "absolute relativism"; that is, each ethnic group is free to interpret God relationally as it sees fit with regard to the Bible as primary resource. For knowledge about God and his workings with humanity, some objectivity is necessary, particularly since all Christians of whatever ethnic group see the Bible as the basic source of God's revelation. And in this area some ethnotheologians propose what can be called a "biblical cultural relativism."[20] This means that the cultural relativism in the Bible is relative to three factors. According to Kraft:

> God conditions his expectations of human beings, in the first place, by making allowances for differences in the endowment and opportunities of the people with whom he is dealing . . . In the second place (and partially overlapping with the first), we see in the Bible a relativism with respect to the extent of the revelational information available to given culture-bound human beings . . . A third aspect of biblical relativism (again partially overlapping with the other two) is the fact that God takes into account the cultures of the people with whom he deals.[21]

This biblical cultural relativism becomes a constant in the way God deals with people who use the Bible as a principal resource. However, the relationship between culture and the Bible must be clearly delimited in order to have correct interpretations of the Bible. Specifically, the issue reduces itself to an interaction which maintains the awareness and integrity of the cultures of the biblical text and of the interpreter. First of all, it is a given that words—as cultural forms—get their meaning from interacting with their contexts. "A cultural form does not have inherent meaning, only perceived meaning—and this is context-specific."[22] That is to say, the biblical text is expressed in specific cultural forms of the period, what we would call literary genres that are, in fact, cultural messages. Yet the determining context of meaning for the biblical author and the modern interpreter is different. This is the question of "the two horizons."

From a cultural-anthropological perspective for determining meaning from the biblical text or symbol, Charles Kraft proposes awareness of three levels of abstraction: the deep level of human universals, the level of world values, and the level of specific customs.[23] For example, the deep level of human universals applies to all cultures at all times, such as love of neighbor (as mandated both in TANAK and the New Testament). The level of world values means that a certain value has currency in most cultures as category of cultural behavior, such as stealing. Finally, at the level of specific custom, for example, stealing a donkey as described in TANAK, there is variety of expression of the human universal and world values. With regard to religiosidad popular, we could see as human universal the relationship with the transcendent; the level of world values as the worship and honoring of God; and the specific cultural level of a given devotional practice, such as the home altar or pilgrimage. Thus when we try to understand the relationship between the Bible and religiosidad popular from the viewpoint of cultural anthropology, we must first recognize and accept the deeper cultural levels in both the Bible and religiosidad popular of relationship with the transcendent and worship of God and see that the specific devotional practice is but a particular cultural expression of these principles.

Other useful insights from cultural anthropology for an understanding of the relationship between the Bible and religiosidad popular are provided by Bruce Malina in his significant monograph *The New Testament World: Insights from Cultural Anthropology*.[24] Though Malina bases his study on the first-century Mediterranean world, the era of the New Testament, the work has relevance for our understanding of religiosidad popular. He begins by positing the value of cultural anthropology for study of the Bible, which is that it asks the "Why?" question of Scripture, whereas most modern methodology (especially the historical-critical method) asks "Who?" "What?" "When?" and "Where?" Malina states:

> To answer a why question in relation to human social behavior, our own culture provides us with a truism as a starting point: All human beings are entirely the same, entirely different, and somewhat the same and somewhat different at the same time. The area of sameness asks why questions about the physical environment and about man as part of that environment: this is nature. The area of difference asks why questions about unique individuals and their unique personal stories: this is person. The area of partial similarity and partial difference asks why questions about the human environment people have developed as the framework or model of their social behavior: this is culture.[25]

Symbolization is endemic to a culture in that the people of a given cultural group share in the significant patterns of the symbolizing process, which the people then absorb and express in their behavior codes: language, customs, and so forth. Cultural anthropology, according to Malina, then has as its focus the formulation of models in order to understand cultures other than our own. There are several models of cultural anthropology, and chief among them are the structural/functionalist, the conflict/coercion, and the symbolic. The symbolic model of cultural anthropology is the most appropriate one for understanding the relationship between the Bible and religiosidad popular. On this point Malina says that a social system of symbols: ". . . acts to establish powerful, pervasive, and long-lasting moods and motivation in people, formulating conceptions of value objects, and clothing these conceptions with such an aura of factuality that the moods and motivations are perceived to be uniquely realistic."[26]

The system of symbols in religiosidad popular would include the meaning, values, and feelings attached to persons and things, including nature, time, space, and events, as the people experiencing them define them. That is, "the symbol gets its range of meaning from shared social expectations . . . much as words get their meaning from the shared social speech system."[27] In effect, the symbolic model in cultural anthropology presupposes that human interactions are generally symbolic interactions—the implications of certain gestures, words, practices, and so forth.

There are at least three insights from cultural anthropology as suggested in Malina's work that can be applied to religiosidad popular as it relates to the Bible. Although Malina discusses his models in context of the first-century Mediterranean world, they may be applicable analogously to the context of twentieth-century Hispanics in the southwestern United States because of certain affinities that exist with the Bible with respect to worldview, relationship to nature, intuitive sense of the transcendent, among others. These areas of analogy are: the individual and the group; the perception of limited good; and kinship and marriage.

THE INDIVIDUAL AND THE GROUP

Twentieth-century Western culture promotes a sort of rugged individualism that translates into a fierce independence allowing one to act in spite of what others say. However, in the first-century Mediterranean world (and in TANAK by implication), there was a reciprocity of belonging and responsibility between the individual and the group. In TANAK before the exilic period, this was generally known as "corporate personality."[28] Cultural anthropology calls this phenomenon a "closed corporate group." In order to know who he or she really is, a person sees himself or herself as interrelated to other persons. There is a feedback on values from others to the individual; because of stated values, the individual's self-perception is dependent on the group's response.[29] In the Hispanic culture of the Southwest, there is a very strong sense of family and community values (based on family, ethnic, historical, and religious concerns) that provides the individual Hispanic a stronger bond of both belief and behavior to the community's value system than to the dominant set of values that are from outside the culture. This gives the Hispanic a sense of belonging and a strong sense of identity.

THE PERCEPTION OF LIMITED GOOD

The first-century Mediterranean world was primarily a peasant society whose main perception was that all goods are limited and there is behavior proper to this perception. Peasant society was a closed system wherein people were aware of their lack of power and influence with regard to the wider society, the "big city," where the elites would not grant power or authority willingly. Thus horizontal relationships assumed priority over vertical ones for meeting the needs of the group. A kind of peer interaction reinforced the significance of shared symbol systems.[30]

Many Hispanics in the Southwest who are practitioners of religiosidad popular come from small pueblos, villages that are constitutive of a peasant society, and often see themselves as powerless with regard to the power elites in the "big city." This tendency toward strengthening horizontal relationships for self-affirmation has an effect on both a religious and social level. God is often referred to in familiar terms, usually called *Diosito, ito* being a diminutive expressing affection. Saints are also often seen as colleagues, with the major difference being that they have intercessory access to God. Saints and personifications are sometimes referred to as *compadre* or *comadre*, as in *mi comadre Doña Sebastiana*, a ritual figure of Holy Week in northern New Mexico. The social dimension of horizontal relationships sees most if not all members of the village as a potential provider of needs, since they are normally referred to as *compadre* or *comadre*.

KINSHIP AND MARRIAGE

"Kinship and its major generating institution, marriage, deal with the meanings and values embodied by persons who are involved in the birth of a child and the process begun by birth."[31] Certainly, for Hispanics the birth of a child is a significant event for both its religious and social values. Baptism becomes predominantly a social event, so much so that on occasion arrangements for the fiesta surrounding the baptismal celebration are settled prior to arrangements with the priest. This may serve to counter the sense of isolation, deprivation, or oppression the Hispanic has felt with regard to the wider society, so the fiesta becomes a modified self-affirmation. The kinship established through sponsorship of a child at baptism and other sacraments is very strong and is known as *compadrazgo*. Because of the kinship bond established through compadrazgo, the compadre and comadre often assume financial as well as religious responsibilities toward the child or person. There is no equivalent in English for the concept, though "coparent" might come close.

There are also notable parallels between the current Hispanic kinship system and that of biblical times, specifically the first-century Mediterranean world. We conclude this from Malina's remarks:

Distinctive features of kinship norms in first century Palestinian society include incest taboos, monogamy, a sort of endogamy, emphasis on the male line of descent, patrilocal marriage, a somewhat extended family living arrangement, the family as a unit of production, emphasis

on family traditions, arranged marriages, geographic and social immo-
bility, ties of affection between brothers and sisters and mothers and
children rather than between husband and wife . . .[32]

Most of these elements have a degree of application to the Hispanic family
in the Southwest. Particularly evident are the extended family and its significance as a socially/religiously functioning unit and a strong emphasis on
family traditions.

Malina discusses three models of marriage strategies in biblical times
from the perspective of cultural anthropology,[33] which may be said to have
some relation to the Hispanic context. I will discuss only two. The first
example is the "conciliatory" model typical of the patriarchal period, where
the female is considered part of the male's honor in that the marriage was
arranged for the father's (patriarch's) benefit. In the Hispanic family, the
female is still to some extent under the control of the father, who often
exercises patriarchy and machismo with regard to his daughters. The second
example, the "aggressive" model, is typical of the pre-exilic Israelite period,
where the women of the tribe were denied to outsiders with the idea that
daughters should marry relatives as close to home as incest rules would
allow. Marriage became a power game among males, with women as the
weapons. In the Hispanic culture, this sense of power among males
expresses itself more in the "rules of the game" set forth by the males.
Often this takes the form of the double standard with regard to sexual
behavior. The Hispanic male is allowed his "affairs," which are forbidden
to the women.

How do these insights from cultural anthropology affect our understanding of religiosidad popular with regard to the Bible? First of all, with regard
to the concept of supracultural, we can say that God is above all cultures
yet perceived by each culture according to its own norms. The perception
of God in Scripture is viewed by the Hispanic especially through the cultural
mediation of religiosidad popular. Second, the model of symbolization best
helps understand religiosidad popular, because Hispanic culture in its religious expression is heavy on symbolism with biblical analogues, as we shall
see later. Third, with regard to the notion of the individual and the group,
the Hispanic sense of religious values is best understood, appreciated, and
critiqued from within the cultural group. In religiosidad popular, the values
expressed within a specific practice – humility, dependence, sorrow, and so
forth – are reinforced and evaluated by fellow practitioners within the
group. Sometimes the objective norm for critique of the value has biblical
origins: A mother accepts her sorrowful lot because of her son's misfortune,
much as La Pietá, the sorrowful mother (or *Nuestra Señora de Dolores* – a
Marian title in religiosidad popular).

Fourth, with regard to perception of the limited good, we note that
horizontal relationships in Hispanic communities are forged through common experiences of joy and suffering. The limited-good theory posits rival-

ries and jealousies within a community for possession of the limited resources, including attention and blessings from God, but at the same time enables the Hispanic practitioners of religiosidad popular to resort to the Bible for a solution or accommodation to these tensions. In religiosidad popular, this horizontal relating is usually done through personalizing and sharing the experience with God or a particular saint. In the Bible we see a great deal of personalizing and sharing by the people with regard to God, especially through prayers of petition, lamentation, thanksgiving, and so forth.

Fifth, in regard to kinship and marriage, popular celebration of the sacraments and other religious rituals usually effects and/or strengthens a strong kinship system that engenders mutual support and affirmation. This would include marriage. There are biblical analogues for this process. For Hispanics the most notable effects of this kinship system are the extended family and strong sense of family traditions. In this context, religiosidad popular can often serve as a means of nourishing these already existing family ties.

Finally, cultural anthropology can serve as a sort of window cleaner that cleans the sometimes smudgy window through which we view religiosidad popular. Hopefully, our vision of Hispanic culture through this discipline can help us understand and appreciate religiosidad popular not only as a legitimate faith-expression of a particular ethnic group but also as a legitimate faith-expression with roots in the Bible.

RECENT BIBLICAL HERMENEUTICAL THEORY

The first step in positing a direct relationship between the Bible and religiosidad popular has been through the discipline of cultural anthropology. Now it remains to clarify that relationship through biblical hermeneutical method.

For well over a century the predominant method of biblical criticism has been the historical-critical method, with its focus on the biblical text. This method tended to ask questions of the text, such as, "How accurate is this manuscript reading in light of other text traditions?" "Which reading is the more authentic?" "What is the literary form, style, context of this particular text?" "What changes have occurred, if any, in the development of the traditions, and what have redactors added throughout the redactional process?"

The disciplines of textual criticism, literary criticism, form criticism, tradition criticism, and redaction criticism as constitutive of the historical critical method developed in order to deal with these questions. Though these basic questions regarding the text were being answered by the historical-critical method, there was a whole new rich avenue of inquiry left unexplored until comparatively recently: the *affective* dimension of the biblical text. The question here is: "How does the biblical text *affect* the reader who helps give it meaning?" After all, the biblical texts were written in order to be read, so the latent presupposition is that the reader is to have some interpretative role with regard to the text.

It is a basic datum that no one method is completely inclusive in interpretation. The rise of new methodologies is an attempt on the part of biblical scholarship to deepen the understanding of the biblical message by first making us aware of the complexities surrounding the communication of that message. As rhetorical criticism[34] emerged to refine the understanding provided by the existing historical-critical method, with its focus on the text, so other new methodologies arose to further expand that understanding by taking into account the involvement of the reader/hearer in interpretation. All the differing methodologies work in conjunction with one another to reach a fuller understanding, for only then can there be integrity in interpretation.

Two of the newer methodologies that supplement the historical-critical method with its focus on the text are structuralism and reader-response criticism, which focus on the reader as interpreter.[35]

STRUCTURALISM

Structuralism as a method generally began a number of years ago to analyze human social phenomena from an anthropological perspective. From there it moved on to other disciplines, including biblical hermeneutics. The presuppositions of structuralism for biblical hermeneutics are basically two. Terence J. Keegan, who wrote a book on recent biblical hermeneutical method, describes them this way:

> A fundamental presupposition that is basic to all structuralist research is the existence of fixed sets of abstract rules which govern all forms of social activity ... For structuralists, all forms of social activity are forms of communication ... Language is simply one of the many forms of communication ... The work of structuralists to date has been largely the establishment of these fixed sets of laws according to which a variety of forms of social activity take place ...
>
> A second presupposition for structuralists, which is usually more basic than the first, is that human beings as such have an innate, genetically transmitted and determined mechanism that acts as a structuring force.[36]

These presuppositions tell us that there are "deep structures" often not realized that are behind all social interactions, and these structures have their fixed rules, which are applicable anytime and anywhere. According to structuralists, the idea is that authors actually utilize deep structures that communicate meaning to the reader rather than to the text. Keegan states: "... most people who write are not the least bit aware of these deep structures that make their writing meaningful, any more than the people who receive them are aware of these deep structures. These deep structures, nevertheless, are operative both in the work of the writer and in the work of the reader . . ."[37]

There are generally three levels of structure. The first level is called "structures of enunciation," those issues that deal with the author's concrete living situation and his purpose for writing. When dealing with a biblical text, this level is usually addressed by the historical critic through form-criticism, tradition-criticism, or whatever branch of the method is called for. The second level of structure is generally called "cultural structures," or the cultural codes of the author's culture—those values and systems that explain the author's background and frame of reference. This level is what cultural anthropology would address, as discussed earlier. The third level of structure, and that proper to structural exegesis, is the level of "deep structures"—fixed structures that are constitutive of human beings everywhere, such as the way stories are told and the existence of certain myths.

These deep structures of narrative and myth function primarily and effectively in the world of symbolism where meaning is frequently more connotive than denotive, referential rather than explicit. The narrative and mythic structures putatively common to all humanity are part of the symbolic world (referential meaning) of semantics, which the structuralists seek to explain.

First there is the question of the deep structure of narrative. The initial presupposition is that all narrative follows essentially the identical structure: the disruption of order, attempt to reestablish order with occasional hindrance, and reestablishment of order. Structuralists say that all narrative, including biblical narrative, follows this pattern. Thus a relatively unsophisticated person reading or hearing a biblical narrative would be able to identify with, if not fully understand, that narrative because of the dynamic of deep structure.

Second, the deep structure of myth is said to be even more profound than the narrative structure, because myths are paradigmatic while narratives are sequential. Narratives have sequence or logic, while myths operate with symbolism that establishes paradigms for thought and action. As Keegan points out:

Quite frequently in biblical narratives one can find mythic structures. What a myth basically does is resolve oppositions. A myth is a way of coping with the fundamental oppositions that one constantly faces in the course of human living . . . The meaning of the myth is to be found entirely in the manner in which the oppositions, the fundamental oppositions, are overcome, fundamental oppositions like life and death, or heaven and earth, or God and man. These are fundamental oppositions that are so radically opposed that there is no middle ground, there is no way logical minds can bring the two together. Myths overcome these oppositions by providing corresponding oppositions, that can be overcome, that do admit of mediation.[38]

In the mythic structure it is important to recognize the proportionality between various pairs of opposites, namely whether or not the opposites can be mediated. For example, the opposites of life and death have no mediation. The structuring of myth attempts to make the nonmediated opposition tolerable. That is to say, it would provide a corresponding opposition that can be mediated, for example, a special act of healing, a "miracle."

In the life of the average, simple person there are many pairs of opposites functioning, especially the forces of good and evil interacting with him or her. According to deep mythic structure, the seemingly irreconcilable opposition between good and evil is overcome through a special mediation, a divine intervention.

Structuralist hermeneutics could be useful in understanding religiosidad popular's relation to the Bible in two ways. First, with regard to the deep structure of narrative, the practitioner of religiosidad popular, with an already established link to the Bible, would be able to identify with the dynamics of the narrative because of the deep structure, if there are clear biblical analogues to the specific practice of religiosidad popular in the first place. Specific examples will be given in subsequent chapters. Second, with regard to the deep structure of myth, there is first the paradigmatic world of symbolism, which is common to both religiosidad popular and mythic structures. The interpretative function is consequently inferential. In the Hispanic realm of experience there are many opposites functioning within the person, especially the struggle between good and evil manifested in various forms. In a particular practice of religiosidad popular, often the apparently irreconcilable opposites—suffering-joy, tension-tranquility, sickness-health—are resolved through mediation, through direct appeal either to God or to the saints. If there are analogues in religiosidad popular, the mythic structures in the Bible serve as models.

READER-RESPONSE CRITICISM

A second recent methodology that focuses on the reader rather than the biblical text and can be useful for understanding the relationship between religiosidad popular and the Bible is called reader-response criticism.[39] Reader-response criticism arose, ironically, in response to the rigid objectivity of the new criticism that was obviously influenced by scientific positivism.[40] One of the principal postulates of reader-response criticism is that "literature deals with human attitudes, with feelings. The result of a literary endeavor is in no way objectifiable."[41] It is impossible, say reader-response critics, to have an absolutely objective interpretation, since all explanations are interpretations. The issue then becomes one of choosing the data and method from which to make interpretations. And since the historical-critical method, in its strive toward objectivity, has neglected the reader in the hermeneutical process, reader-response criticism seeks to fill the void. Reader-response critics hold that there is no single objective meaning to the biblical text that is available to all. The biblical text has potentialities, a sort of "semantic universe" surrounding it, which make various interpretations possible. Thus the author provides a meaning for one generation, and readers of the same and subsequent generations can provide others.

Another basic presupposition of reader-response criticism is that a literary work is a "bi-polar virtual entity." As Keegan puts it:

A literary work is a bi-polar virtual entity. A virtual entity is something which is capable of existing but which does not yet exist. Only when the two poles of a literary work are both operative does a literary work come into being. Every truly literary work has both an artistic pole and an aesthetic pole. The artistic pole is the artistic creation of the author ... The other pole, the aesthetic pole, is the work of the reader. Both of these poles are necessary. Without both of them operating, the literary work is simply a potentiality. Its potentiality becomes an actuality when both of these poles are operating, when a reader picks up the work of an author and actually reads it. In actually reading it, it comes into being. It is real, it has meaning, and it does something.[42]

The key factor in this *tolle, lege* scenario is that the reader's imagination is thereby activated, and from the semantic universe of the words in the text the reader as artist draws and gives meaning to the text. The potentiality is thus reduced to actuality. This process is used, above all, in narrative, where the author often leaves gaps to be filled by the reader. This results in the dynamic interchange of assumptions made by the reader which are challenged by the text which results in further assumptions, and so on. The reader thus actually becomes involved in the interpretation of the text.[43]

How does this brief glimpse into reader-response criticism help us understand the relationship between religiosidad popular and the Bible? Again, it is possible only if there are biblical analogues in the specific practice of religiosidad popular. First of all, in reader-response criticism, literature deals with human attitudes and feelings. The Hispanic practitioner of religiosidad popular is basically an affective person and would thus respond to literature, particularly biblical literature, in that fashion. Second, in reader-response criticism the literary work, in this case the Bible, is a bi-polar entity that must have its two poles interacting simultaneously in order to exist. In the context of religiosidad popular and the Bible, these poles are the biblical author and the Hispanic reader or hearer who is also a practitioner of religiosidad popular. In the reading or hearing of a particular biblical text, especially narrative, the already predisposed imagination of the Hispanic practitioner of religiosidad popular is activated into entering and interacting with a symbolic, semantic world of the text, filling in gaps in meaning through assumptions which are made and challenged.

A similar argument from a different perspective may be made by referring to the discussion of Raul Vidales, who speaks of the function of sacraments among Mexicans by showing parallels in the Old Testament. He says that the "sacramental signs," such as salvation, messianism, and so forth, though functional in the present, have a future orientation and indicate possibilities for the messianic future because they have "polyvalent meaning" (*significado plurivalente*)[44] in the sense that with the experience of the sacrament, the recipient can draw one of many possible meanings that are particularly applicable to one's personal life.

Another connection between religiosidad popular and the Bible, with possible inferences for the hermeneutical methods of structuralism and reader-response criticism, is made by the Mexican theologian Raul Duarte Castillo, who states that there is a certain adaptation of religious imagery that occurs between the Bible and other cultures that share the religious "world imagery of the Bible," for example, the Hispanic culture.[45] Some examples of this would be the image of God as father, because the God of Israel/Hispanics is seen in familiar terms; the image of the Sinai covenant, because it is bilateral and conditional, and has the implication of mutuality of obligation.

Yet a third observation, by Javier Lozano Barragán, a Mexican theologian, with regard to religiosidad popular from which we can infer a link to reader-response criticism and the structuralist approach to biblical hermeneutics, is that religious expressions in general and Mexican religiosidad popular in particular have their fundamental expressions in myth, legend, and the narrative.[46]

FOUR DEVOTIONS OF RELIGIOSIDAD POPULAR FOR ANALYSIS

It remains now to specify certain devotional practices of religiosidad popular with a high probability of links with TANAK. The biblical approach that ensues will adopt the following method. First, seek biblical analogues with the devotional practice, grounding the analogues, from the viewpoint of the biblical text, through aspects of the historical-critical method. Second, attempt to strengthen the analogues from the viewpoint of religiosidad popular, supported by insights from cultural anthropology, structuralism, reader-response criticism, and language theory. Third, suggest pastoral implications through which Hispanic devotional piety can be better understood and appreciated for enriching life and liturgy.

The four devotions I have chosen for special study are as heterogeneous in their expression as the reasons for their choice. They are: Ash Wednesday, the *Quinceañera*, the home altar, and the *Penitentes*. Three of the four are practical realities in most of the Hispanic parishes of the Southwest, and one is virtually universal in Hispanic Catholicism.

Ash Wednesday is an official celebration in the church's liturgical year, opening the penitential season of Lent that prepares us for the drama of Holy Week, the death and resurrection of Jesus. Anyone who has ever worked in a Hispanic parish or witnessed an Ash Wednesday service in a predominantly Hispanic parish knows that for many Hispanic practitioners of religiosidad popular, receiving the ashes is more significant personally than participating in the accompanying Mass, let alone receiving the Eucharist. The Quinceañera, also very common in most Hispanic parishes of the Southwest, is a rite of passage for a young girl celebrating her fifteenth birthday. This celebration takes on important religious and social significance. The home altar, in my estimation, is one of the devotions in religiosidad popular that best represents a personal covenant relationship with God without the mediation of the institutional church. The Penitentes are a brotherhood, rooted principally in northern New Mexico, with a special devotion to the suffering Christ. My paternal grandfather and other relatives in northern New Mexico were Penitentes, and as a youth I was often fascinated by accounts of this particular group. In addition, this devotion represents a good example of the critical principle used in biblical studies called *Ortsgebundenheit*, namely the fact that a particular religious tradition is bound to a given locale.[47] In this case, the fixed locale is primarily northern New Mexico and southern Colorado.

However, before we actually begin the analysis of these four practices of religiosidad popular according to the method proposed above, it is first necessary to deal with the issue of divine revelation, since revelation is the master key which unlocks the treasures of the relationship between the Bible and religiosidad popular.

3

Revelation and Religiosidad Popular

CHURCH TEACHING ON REVELATION

One of the most basic issues that confronts a deeply religious person is the understanding and developing of a relationship with God. That relationship is predicated on communication that purports to let the person know the self-manifestation of God and his plan of salvation for humanity, opaquely in history and creation and clearly in the person and message of Jesus Christ as found in the Word of God. This predicated communication is what Christian theology would call revelation. The problem posed by revelation is essentially that of: How does God reveal himself? And what is the content of that revelation? Responses to these queries will take us into the nature and function of revelation. After discussion of revelation in general, with specific reference to the Bible, I will examine the hypothesis that religiosidad popular has a highly probable claim of legitimacy as a locus of divine revelation.

The basic point of reference for discussing revelation from a theological and biblical perspective is the Vatican II Constitution on Divine Revelation, known as *Dei Verbum* and promulgated on November 18, 1965. The document states that the object of divine revelation is God's self-revelation and his revelation of the mystery of his will regarding human salvation, which he has given through Jesus Christ (2). History is a principal forum where a revelatory interaction takes place between deeds and words (2). The council admits that God can be known in creation and through reason (3, 6), but is known more specifically through Scripture. The Christian economy focuses on Jesus Christ as ". . . the mediator and the sum total of Revelation" (2). As Jesus is definitively manifested in the New Testament and is understood to be implied in the Old Testament, this revelation in Jesus ". . . will never pass away; and no new public revelation is to be expected before the glorious manifestation of Our Lord, Jesus Christ" (4). God's self-revelation is thus an incarnational revelation: made manifest through history, creation, and above all, through Jesus Christ as known

34

through the Scriptures. The content of revelation is the message of salvation, what we Catholics would call our deposit of faith.

The council document discusses in chapter 2 the transmission of divine revelation, that is, the specifics of how divine revelation is made known to all. Even though the council fathers are specific about the orderly transmission of revelation from God through Jesus to the apostles and their successors, the bishops (7), nonetheless they allow for the broader concept of the church, the "People of God" (8), serving as the recipient and interpreter of revelation. What is astonishing in the context of this hierarchical view of the transmission of revelation is the council's apparent openness to the development of revelation and the variety of interpretative fonts. For example:

> The Tradition that comes from the apostles *makes progress in the Church* with the help of the Holy Spirit. There is a *growth in insight* into the realities and words that are being passed on. This comes about in various ways. It comes through the contemplation and study of believers who ponder these things in their hearts . . . It comes from the intimate sense of spiritual realities which they experience. And it comes from the preaching of those who have received, along with their right of succession in the episcopate, the sure charism of truth. Thus, as the centuries go by, *the Church is always advancing toward the plenitude of divine truth*, until eventually the words of God are fulfilled in her.
>
> . . . Thus *God*, who spoke in the past, *continues to converse* with the spouse of his beloved Son. And the Holy Spirit . . . leads believers to the full truth . . . (8, italics mine).

Tradition is here used in the sense of forming part of the sacred deposit of the Word of God, namely the message of revelation.

One can almost sense in *Dei Verbum* the struggle that may have gone on among the council bishops when formulating the document. Here the progressivists score a point, there the traditionalists score another. We can detect in the document a sort of schizophrenia regarding the identity of the authentic recipients and transmitters of divine revelation. Paragraphs 9 and 10 promote the idea that Scripture and Tradition form the one deposit of the Word of God. Paragraph 9 postulates the bishops as the authentic recipients and transmitters, whereas paragraph 10 specifically mentions the *church* — in its broad sense as promoted by the council to mean not just the bishops — as the authentic recipient and transmitter. Also in paragraph 10 the document states emphatically that the authentic interpretation of the Word of God ". . . has been entrusted to the living teaching office of the Church alone." Yet it is clear that ". . . this magisterium is not superior to the Word of God, but is its servant." According to *Dei Verbum*, the authentic recipients and transmitters of divine revelation are sacred

Tradition, sacred Scripture, and the magisterium of the church. Within this triadic arrangement, the authority of sacred Tradition can claim a modicum of independence from the magisterium—a point I shall pursue later.

Obviously the most important member in this troika of revelatory elements is sacred Scripture, which for Christians includes the Old and New Testaments. All Scripture, to be properly understood, needs interpretation. Prominence is given to seeking the intention of the author if one is to determine what God wished to communicate to us (12). Thus the hermeneutical concern in *Dei Verbum* turns out to be twofold: What did the biblical text mean then? What does it mean now? We answer the latter only by dealing with the former. Hence knowledge of literary forms and other exegetical tools becomes necessary for legitimate interpretation. The document states clearly that:

> Rightly to understand what the sacred author wanted to affirm in his work, due attention must be paid both to the customary and characteristic patterns of perception, speech and narrative which prevailed at the age of the sacred writer, and to the conventions which the people of his time followed in their dealings with one another.
>
> But since sacred Scripture must be read and interpreted with its divine authorship in mind, no less attention must be devoted to the context and unity of the whole of Scripture, taking into account the Tradition of the *entire* Church and the analogy of faith, *if we are to derive their true meaning* from the sacred texts. It is the task of the exegetes to work, according to these rules, towards a better understanding and explanation of the meaning of sacred Scripture in order that their research may help the Church to form a firmer judgement (12, italics mine).

In sum, the document *Dei Verbum* presents us with the following understanding of terms.

Revelation: The self-manifestation of God and his plan of salvation for humanity, opaquely in history and creation and clearly in the person and message of Jesus Christ (2–6) as found in the Word of God.

Tradition: Both sacred Scripture and sacred Tradition form the Word of God. By Tradition is meant transmission of the apostolic teaching by means other than the inspired books. Tradition includes all that helps the people of God live in holiness and grow in faith (8). This Tradition grows and develops with the help of the Holy Spirit, providing new insight for subsequent generations through contemplation and study, experience of spiritual realities, and preaching from those who have received "the sure charism of truth" (8).

Hermeneutics: Hermeneutics is the discipline of interpretation. *Dei Verbum* states clearly that the magisterium, as official interpreter of Scripture, is not superior to the Word of God, but is its servant (10). In fact, there are three interdependent elements involved in an authentic understanding of divine revelation: Tradition, Scripture, and magisterium. "... one of them cannot stand without the others. Working together, each in its own way under the action of the Holy Spirit, they all contribute effectively to the salvation of souls" (10).

In these statements we have a clear distinction between Tradition and magisterium, the former being the apostolic teaching guarded by the entire people of God, and the latter being the episcopal interpretation of that teaching. However, the document seems to imply that there is equal responsibility among hierarchy and nonhierarchy as church to "contribute effectively to the salvation of souls" under the guidance of the Holy Spirit. We can infer that guardianship of the apostolic teaching, attributed to the entire church, means understanding it, and a priori interpreting it in order to understand it. The key question here becomes: Is there an equality of authenticity in the interpretation of Scripture between hierarchy and nonhierarchy when it contributes effectively to the salvation of souls? The answer is more complex than a simple yes or no.

Chapter 3 of *Dei Verbum* deals with the human dimension in the writing of the sacred books, emphasizing the need to take into account the meaning of the sacred authors through discernment of literary forms and other aspects of the historical-critical method (12). The exegetes are given a further task of taking into account the Tradition of the *entire* church and the analogy of faith to help in the better understanding of Scriptures. If we could point to something that is truly significant in this document, it is the notion that authentic interpretation of the Scriptures is a *process*— suggested throughout the document and particularly in paragraph 21— engaged in through cooperation of bishops, exegetes, and faithful. But even while conceding with the right hand participation to the wider church in the process of interpreting, the document qualifies with the left hand by insisting that the bishops are the sole authentic (that is, juridically authoritative) interpreters of divine revelation. There seems to be room in the document for an expanded view of revelation.

FOUNDATIONAL AND DEPENDENT REVELATION

Our discussion of revelation now brings us to a clarification of terminology. The major distinction occurs between what we could call "official" and "unofficial" or "public" and "private" revelation. We need one term to indicate the kind of revelation that was given to Israel in biblical times, was completed in Christ, and has thus become normative for the church. This would constitute what the New Testament and church documents refer to as the "deposit of faith." This is what *Dei Verbum* calls "public" revelation (4).

There is also the need to consider a wider sense of revelation that is outside of official channels. *Dei Verbum*, in light of the total conciliar documentation, speaks of church as being more extensive than just hierarchy when dealing with revelation. The interesting distinction between Tradition and magisterium, and the emphatic statement that magisterium is subordinate to the Word of God (10), indicate that the conciliar bishops were recognizing, at least tacitly, the existence of a church interpretation of the Word of God that is beyond simple episcopal authority alone. The *sensus fidelium* and the input from professional exegetes seem to me to provide the raw material for this wider notion of church interpreting revelation. What term do we use, in contrast to public revelation, to designate the revelation proper to this wider notion of church?

Seminal theologians have struggled with the issue. Paul Tillich, in an attempt to understand the two kinds of revelation, suggests the terms "original" and "dependent." Tillich's original revelation is what we would call the deposit of faith. Furthermore, he states that, "The divine Spirit, illuminating believers individually and as a group, brings their cognitive reason into revelatory correlation with the event on which Christianity is based. *This leads to a broader view of revelation* in the life of the Christian. *A dependent revelatory situation exists* in every moment in which the divine Spirit grasps, shakes, and moves the human spirit"[1] (italics mine). Tillich thus recognizes the broader revelation, which he calls "dependent" because it is dependent on the originary revelation.

Theologian John Macquarrie speaks of "classic" or "primordial" revelation which he says is, ". . . A definitive disclosive experience of the holy granted to the founder or founders of the community, becomes as it were the paradigm for experiences of the holy in that community."[2] By contrast, "A revelation that has the power to found a community of faith becomes fruitful in that community, and is, so to speak, repeated or reenacted in the experience of the community, thus becoming normative for the experience of the community."[3] For Macquarrie the terms are classic/primordial and repetitive revelations. The repetitive aspect is the generational reinterpretation. He concludes: "Each generation must appropriate the tradition, and in order to do this it has to interpret the ancient formula, or whatever it may be, into its own categories of thought."[4] The generational reinterpretation of primordial revelation, according to Macquarrie, is mediated through Scripture and tradition.[5]

Finally, theologian Gerald O'Collins presents what I think is the most appropriate distinction between the two aspects of divine revelation under discussion so far, namely foundational revelation and dependent revelation.

> The first Christians, and above all the apostles, experienced and testified to the *foundational* history of revelation and salvation. These founding fathers and founding mothers enjoyed the once-and-for-all experience of living intimately with Jesus, encountering him in his risen glory and becoming the basic witness to the resurrection. Revelation and salvation did not grind to a halt at the end of the apostolic

era, but continued and continues in dependence upon the unique and normative apostolic experience of and witness to Jesus Christ. Thus the religious experience of post-apostolic Christians constitutes a *dependent* history of revelation and salvation. They know this experience of the divine self-communication to be tied to and derived from a series of historical events and persons—specifically, Jesus of Nazareth and the events in which he was involved.[6]

Thus in further discussion "foundational" revelation is what we generally refer to as the deposit of faith, the revelation that Tillich calls "original," Macquarrie calls "primordial," and *Dei Verbum* calls "public." The wider revelation we shall call "dependent," together with Tillich and O'Collins. This dependent revelation, since it is derivative from the foundational, develops as the generational reinterpretation of that foundational revelation, and so is a deepening of the understanding that already exists.

One major question regarding revelation remains, and that is: How does one discern this authentic post-apostolic dependent revelation? Basically, the criteria for discernment are two: the Bible and Tradition. With regard to the Bible as criterion for discernment of revelation, I am referring primarily to interpretative method. In that regard, we note that in addition to the historical-critical method as interpretative tool of the text, there are also the additional methods of structuralism and reader-response criticism, which take into account the receptivity/interpretation of the reader or hearer. The historical-critical method is more conducive to discerning the meaning of the biblical text concerning foundational revelation, whereas that methodology that takes the reader or hearer of the biblical text into account as legitimate interpreter is more conducive to dependent revelation. That is to say, the notion of revelation that is broader than the foundational revelation, which is fixed in the creeds and professions of faith, is dependent revelation, with its more appropriate, and no less valid, criteria of interpretation.

The second criterion of discernment for dependent revelation is Tradition, that apostolic teaching entrusted to the broader church (the people of God) and independent of magisterium as described in *Dei Verbum*. This Tradition, which has roots in culture, as pointed out in *Ad Gentes* (11), is constantly growing in insight, as *Dei Verbum* indicates. And it is the church as entire people of God under the guidance of the Holy Spirit that gives legitimacy of interpretation to dependent revelation. The guidance of the Holy Spirit can sometimes come in the form of scholarly work from the exegetes and direction from the magisterium.

When comparing foundational revelation and dependent revelation, it is of crucial importance to see the relationship between the two. Post-apostolic dependent revelation does not provide new truths. All truth necessary for salvation is already present in the foundational revelation. *Dei Verbum* is clear on this. Rather, dependent revelation is a deeper realization

of what is already present in foundational revelation. It is the organic out-
growth of living foundational revelation situated in a concrete historical
and cultural context. There is no arbitrary designation of something as
revelation, foundational or dependent. Criteria are always present. It is the
relationship of each revelatory element to both Scripture and Tradition, as
developed by the criteria for discernment, that essentially distinguishes true
religion from superstition.

On a contemporary note, the Puebla document recognizes on the part
of practitioners of religiosidad popular the probability of intuiting God's
self-revelation, or, in other words, the probability of understanding and
interpreting dependent revelation.

The faith of a people who practice religiosidad popular sharing this
unofficial knowledge of God's self-revelation is recognized by the final
Puebla document.

> At its core the religiosity of the people is a storehouse of values that
> offer the answers of Christian wisdom to the great questions of life.
> The Catholic wisdom of the common people is capable of fashioning
> a vital synthesis. It creatively combines the divine and the human,
> Christ and Mary, spirit and body, communion and institution, person
> and community, faith and homeland, intelligence and emotion. This
> wisdom is a Christian humanism that radically affirms the dignity of
> every person as a child of God, establishes a basic fraternity, teaches
> people how to encounter nature and understand work, and provides
> reasons for joy and humor even in the midst of a very hard life. For
> the common people this wisdom is also a principle of discernment
> and an *evangelical instinct* through which they *spontaneously sense* when
> the Gospel is served in the Church and when it is emptied of content
> and stifled by other interests (448, italics mine).

This *evangelical instinct* mentioned by the Puebla document has its parallel in Hispanic practitioners of religiosidad popular with whom I have
worked in the past. The phenomenon I call "intuitive insight" consists
ordinarily of elderly Hispanic devotees of devotional piety, usually unsophisticated and sometimes illiterate, who offer insights into a biblical passage that could be the envy of a professional exegete. How can one explain
this, given that the principal hermeneutical tools for these individuals are
not the various facets of the historical-critical method but rather personal
reflections on a specific biblically based devotional practice with implications for one's personal life? These hermeneutical tools are clearly elements
of structuralism and reader-response criticism. My experience with the Penitentes led me to this conclusion. There seems to be a certain indefinable
intuitive insight into Scripture among practitioners of religiosidad popular
that is somehow revelatory of God's salvific will. This intuitive insight can

be considered dependent revelation insofar as it is related to Scripture and Tradition, as indicated above.

A second problem often encountered in the tension between the official and unofficial with regards to revelation is the assumption that true revelation comes only through official channels, for example the assumption that the media of revelation are "controlled" by the official church through her magisterium. The problem is that a universal claim to the interpretation of God's will always and everywhere is often limited by the geography, history, culture, thought patterns, and worldview of the official interpreters. Failure to take into account these limitations often results in overstatement and loss of credibility, which thus provides motive for unofficial interpretations. The problem of the credibility of official church statements is best handled, as is now frequently the case, by an official acknowledgment of limits. As it turns out, the church is one of the few voices, at times the only voice, that speak out against injustice wherever in the world it exists. But this "prophetic" voice comes in the framework of the church acting as a moral agent exercising responsibility to humanity, and not as the singular, univocal spokesperson for the deity. Thus there needs to be mutual understanding between adherents of official and unofficial interpreters of revelation as to what their proper roles are. There needs to be mutual respect and understanding between strict adherents of foundational revelation and practitioners of dependent revelation.

THE NATURE OF REVELATION

The clarification of roles regarding the interpretation of divine will may begin with an exploration of the "What?" question. What is the nature (and by implication content) of divine revelation? It is difficult to avoid all ambiguity when trying to deal objectively with the nature of revelation, for who can honestly and legitimately claim to know God's mind and prove it beyond the shadow of a doubt? We are faced with a problematic situation that is clearly articulated by Avery Dulles.

The term "revelation" does not appear in the creeds and is not central in the Scriptures. Treatises on revelation did not begin to be written until the Enlightenment period, in controversies with the Deists. But since that time theologians have recognized that an implicit doctrine of revelation underlies every major theological understanding. The great theological disputes turn out, upon reflection, to rest on different understandings of revelation, often simply taken for granted. The controversies that have raged in our own century about the divinity of Christ, the inerrancy of the Bible, the infallibility of the Church, secular and political theology, and the value of other religions would be unintelligible apart from the varying convictions about revelation.[7]

We have from the outset a realization that understanding revelation as a common thread of the theological enterprise is at best ambiguous. Everyone seems to take for granted what it means, but very few bother to explain it. This results in a confused state of affairs.

There are many significant approaches to the study of the nature of revelation in the Bible, for example the etymological approach.[8] But because of the limited scope of this study, I will restrict the investigation to those areas which, in my judgment, most successfully represent an effective interaction between revelation and religiosidad popular. These three areas are tradition, history, and symbol.

TRADITION

To understand the nature of revelation through tradition one must first grasp the distinction between *traditio* and *traditum*. The former is the process of handing down and the latter is the content of what is handed down.[9] In an article on revelation through tradition, Douglas Knight speaks of tradition as being produced by the people engaged in the many aspects of life, a kind of interaction between the *traditio* and the *traditum*. The process of tradition involves people actively. He says: ". . . for while the tradition preserved the memory of the past it is also subject to growth and change at the hands of new generations who face new situations that require reconsideration of their heritage."[10]

In the tradition process, both memory and reinterpretation are crucial elements in the dynamics of revelation, because revelation is more than just a theological matter. It touches upon the phenomenological aspects of a people's view of reality that conditions their perception of God and their interaction with him. People tend to remember in their traditions significant experiences (either positive or negative), and the significance of that memory has new and reinforced meaning for later generations. Each generation reinterprets for itself the contemporary significant meaning of its collective memory of the tradition. We see this process operative in the TANAK prophetic tradition. For example, Amos (5:18–20) speaks of the *yôm YHWH*, the Day of the Lord, as being a time of negative judgment for Israel. In the earlier stages of the tradition, the *yôm YHWH* signified a day of hope and prosperity.[11] Amos took an existing tradition and reinterpreted it—to the point of reversing its original meaning—in order for that tradition to have significance for his generation.

The traditions of a people include both a process and a content, the former being reinterpretation and the latter being memory. What is remembered as revelatory content is Yahweh's message. Thus revelation through tradition is seen as an ongoing experience, or in Knight's phrase, a "durative confrontation" between Yahweh and his people. That is to say, the memory of a meaningful experience, positive or negative, keeps alive the manifested expression of God's revelation in a particular point in time and is reinterpreted by succeeding generations.

One possible difficulty with the revelation-in-tradition concept as discussed above is a question regarding the content of the tradition. How accurate is the memory to be handed down? Because of the memory's inherent linkage to experience, which is variable, and a people's need to share in that experience, the revelatory aspect of memory's content must be flexible, since it is reinterpreted by succeeding generations, thus making revelation patently confessional in character. Perhaps the most obvious expression of this phenomenon is memory as *Vergegenwärtigung*, or "re-presentation," "actualization" of a significant event, usually within a cultic context.[12] Douglas Knight explains:

> the essence of "Vergegenwärtigung" . . . is rather to create a situation in which the people of a new generation can feel affected by the past events, can realize the implications for their own lives, can open themselves to the continued impact of previous revelation. But for this to be effected, interpretation geared to the new situation was mandatory, and through accumulation of such interpretations the tradition itself grew.[13]

Finally, as Knight points out,[14] it is important to bear in mind that revelation occurs not "as" tradition—in a sense identified with it—not "in" tradition—as though some ready commodity, but rather "through" tradition. This prepositional precision is necessary in order to underscore the complexity surrounding the nature of revelation with reference to tradition. The significance of the preposition "through" indicates three things. First, tradition provides the structures necessary to understand revelation as revelation. Second, tradition is the significant life experience that becomes revelatory. Third, tradition is the channel by which the *traditum* is made available to subsequent generations. Consequently, we see revelation through tradition as a dynamic, reciprocal, ongoing interaction between Yahweh and his people.

HISTORY

The idea of revelation through history in the Bible[15] has been quite prominent on the theological scene for at least a generation. The major proponent in the United States has been G. Ernest Wright, primarily through his book *God Who Acts: Biblical Theology as Recital*,[16] and in Europe, Wolfhart Pannenberg, through his work *Revelation as History*.[17] Basically, the argument states that God manifests himself through history because history is the chief medium of divine revelation. One of the major critics of this revelation-through-history approach has been James Barr, who has consistently denied that God is active (revelatory) only in historical deeds.[18]

Recently the notion of revelation through history has been rehabilitated by biblical scholar Werner Lemke.[19] He reiterates some of the criticisms by stating that the two major problems with the revelation-through-history approach are that it is too one-sided and ambiguous. It is too one-sided because it overlooks God's revelatory activity through nature, as seen biblically in the opening chapters of Genesis, the creation hymns of Deutero-Isaiah, some of the Psalms, and above all the wisdom literature. The ambiguity of the revelation-through-history approach is seen primarily in four areas. First, there is ambiguity in the definition of key terms such as "revelation" and "history." The Bible has no term for "history" as such, and "revelation" as a biblical concept has many dimensions that are not adequately covered by terms such as the Hebrew *galah* or the Greek *apokalupto*. Second, there is lack of clarity in ontological and theological assumptions. For example, what is meant precisely by a God who acts? Third, proponents of the position are often descriptive when they should be confessional. Fourth, there is the problematic distinction between actual and confessed history. That is, what did God actually do, and what is he believed to have done?

Regarding this last point, Lemke has an interesting observation that, in my judgment, despite the criticisms justly rehabilitates the concept of revelation through history on a limited scale. Choosing a specific instance of divine intervention in history, he wonders what God did regarding the fall of Jericho when the biblical account says one thing and compelling archaeological evidence says another. Has archaeology done away with the notion of God's action in history? Not in the least, Lemke contends.

> While we may no longer be able to understand God's activity in this instance on the basis of a literal reading of the biblical account, it is possible to understand it in more subtle ways by *not confining the locus of revelation to the objective facticity of the events as narrated in the Bible* ... To the extent that this series of events in the complex transmission process of the story did take place in actual history, and to the extent that it was *in some sense* also divinely induced and/or guided, we may speak of it as revelation through history. In view of the predominance of the *interpretative work in this story*, one could equally well speak of revelation through tradition or story[20] (italics mine).

Thus revelation through history, in Lemke's view, is not limited to external events but must include the process of interpretation and appropriation as well. This approach to understanding the nature of revelation through history by allowing the revelation to occur in the interpretation is well handled by the biblical hermeneutical theory of reader-response criticism discussed earlier.

SYMBOL

Revelation through symbol presents more of a problem because of the multifaceted dimensions of symbolic understanding. So much has been written on symbolism from a variety of perspectives that no attempt will be made here to be exhaustive, only to be illuminative, thus citing only those authors whose insights into symbolism and biblical revelation are both pertinent and useful.

In this regard we have an important contribution by Avery Dulles on the revelatory aspect of symbol that could be translated directly into the biblical context and indirectly into the ambience of religiosidad popular. Acknowledging the work of his predecessors in the field of symbolism and revelation, Dulles begins by clarifying his terms. For him, "A symbol is a sign pregnant with a plenitude of meaning which is evoked rather than explicitly stated."[21] This means, first of all, that surrounding a symbol is a whole field of semantic energy whose meaning can be tapped into. The "tapping into" this semantic energy is the function of hermeneutics. Secondly, the evocation of meaning means that knowledge of the symbol itself demands some kind of involvement by the participant. No passive observation is possible.

Although the usual linkage is between symbol and language, Dulles is correct in not limiting symbolism to the literary sphere as far as revelation is concerned. For him, historical personages, natural objects, visible artifacts, and dreams can all be symbolic. It is significant to note that these nonliterary elements are also present in religiosidad popular.[22]

As mentioned above, one of the elements of symbol—and in my judgment one of the most crucial—is the participatory dimension of its knowledge. A symbol is self-involving. "It [symbol] speaks to us only insofar as it lures us to situate ourselves mentally within the universe of meaning and value which it opens up to us."[23] Because of the involvement of the knower as a person, a transformation takes place in the sense that the symbol shifts our awareness and changes our values. In addition, the symbol has a strong influence on behavior, in that it can appeal to hidden energy resources of activity and response; for example, a country's flag, which can mobilize the energy of a nation. Finally, a symbol involves greater participation by opening up the horizon of possibilities that can precipitate one into different kinds of action, whether for good or for evil, depending upon the motivational impact of the symbol itself. This process of involvement, influence on values, transformation, and opening up further horizons is the revelatory dimension of symbol.

THE FUNCTION OF REVELATION

Thus far we have discussed the nature of revelation as perceived in tradition, history, and symbol in an attempt to determine what revelation is. Now we shall try to see how it functions—our "How?" question. The primary function of revelation is to communicate understanding. Without this communication, history, tradition, and symbol have no revelatory significance. The following general remarks deal with both foundational and dependent revelation, since their functions are the same.

As commonly accepted, foundational revelation as a form of communication has a threefold expression in Christianity: to ground the faith of the Christian, to direct the mission of the church, and to undergird theological argument. Traditionally, there have been problems in understanding the relationship between revelation and these three functions. With regard to faith and revelation, there is often tension that opposes them, but that relationship should be viewed as complementary. As Dulles puts it: "Faith, however, is a stretching forth of the mind toward an insight not given, or not clearly given. Faith, as a kind of trustful probing, animates the quest for revelation; it sustains the process of discovery."[24] With regard to the direction of its mission, which may be questioned, the church in its appeal to revelation ". . . turns to the symbolic sources of its own life and submits to the direction they give, confident that in so doing it is being faithful to the God who reveals."[25] With regard to the undergirding of a theological argument that may lack authority, the church accepts as normative the sources, symbols, and traditions of interpretation as it elucidates revelation.

These, then, are the three traditional functions of revelation operative in the contemporary church: grounding the faith of the Christian, directing the mission of the church, and undergirding theological argument. All are part of foundational revelation. In our consideration of the function of dependent revelation—namely religiosidad popular—we see these three traditional functions overtly operative. However, in order to understand the function of revelation as faith-grounding in religiosidad popular, we must further consider a more basic function, which is the act of understanding itself. Our guide in this consideration is Paul Ricoeur, whose recent impact on biblical scholarship through his language theory is providing significant hermeneutical insight.[26]

Ricoeur states that revelation is not formulated dogma that is subordinated and derived, but rather is *faith-discourse*, which makes it pluralistic, polysemic, and analogical.[27] That is to say, the Bible as principal font of revelation may be taken primarily as faith-discourse capable of multilevel interpretations. Prophecy, narrative, wisdom, and other literary genres are different ways that faith-discourse expresses itself as revelatory. These revelatory categories of faith-discourse in the Bible allow for certain directions of investigation. According to Ricoeur, several directions are charted. First, "A hermeneutic of revelation must give priority to those modalities of discourse that are most originary within the language of a community of faith: consequently, those expressions by means of which the members of that community first interpret their experience for themselves and for others [must be considered originary]."[28] This means that narrative traditions, as memory experience of a people, can be considered as originary within the language of a faith community, since these tradition-memories are constitutive of intergenerational dialogue among a people.

Ricoeur also holds that, ". . . if the forms of religious discourse are so pregnant with meaning, the notion of revelation may no longer be formulated in a uniform and monotonous fashion which we presuppose when we speak of the biblical revelation."[29] The inescapable conclusion is that one can arrive at a "polysemic" understanding—that is, a plurality of meanings—of revelation in the Bible. This means that if, as we postulate, certain forms of revelatory discourse in the Bible are more appropriate at certain points in history than others—for example, prophecy during the monarchical period, wisdom literature and apocalyptic in the postexilic period—then we can say that divine revelation can also be manifested today in narrative discourse, or through the traditions of a people, as would be the case with religiosidad popular.

How then do we deal with the hermeneutic (understanding) of revelation? Ricoeur deals with preparatory concepts as prerequisites which provide for greater understanding in the encounter between text and reader.[30] Easily the most significant of these preparatory concepts for understanding revelation is ". . . the shaping of discourse through the operation of literary genres such as narration, fiction, the essay, etc. By producing discourse as such and such a genre, the composition codes assign to works of discourse that unique configuration we call a style."[31] This means that the shaping of the discourse, which Ricoeur calls "the work," is basically a faith-discourse that finds expression in literary styles peculiar to a given group interpreting a text. In the case of religiosidad popular, the literary style of "narrative"— or more correctly, the traditions in religiosidad popular—would be part of this faith-discourse. Revelation is, in light of Ricoeur's observation on understanding, primarily a faith-discourse that is the communication and understanding of expressions believed to have been effected by God in some way, and with a capability of multilevel interpretations—whether in tradition or history or symbol.[32]

RELIGIOSIDAD POPULAR AS LOCUS OF DIVINE REVELATION

Having discussed the nature and function of revelation, we are now in a position to assert that religiosidad popular is itself a locus of divine revelation. We have seen above the revelatory possibility of tradition, history, and symbol as applicable to the Bible. Tradition, history, and symbol are also culturally constitutive elements of religiosidad popular and therefore have revelatory potential. The Second Vatican Council, in its document *Ad Gentes Divinitus* (Decree on the Church's Missionary Activity), affirmed the revelatory potential of cultures.

The Church must be present to these groups through those of its members who live among them or have been sent to them . . . In order to bear witness to Christ, fruitfully, they should establish relationships of respect and love with those men, they should acknowledge themselves as members of the group in which they live, and through the various undertakings and affairs of human life they should share in their social and cultural life. *They should be familiar with their national and religious traditions and uncover with gladness and respect those seeds of the Word which lie hidden among them.* They must look to the profound transformation which is taking place among nations and work hard so that modern man is . . . aroused to desire, even more intensely, that love and truth which have been revealed by God (11, italics mine).

Second, we have seen the revelatory function of faith-discourse as an attempt to understand divine communication. Because of culturally constitutive elements, this faith-discourse is polysemous in character—capable of multilevel interpretation. Religiosidad popular, by its nature as cultural phenomenon with elements of tradition, history, and symbol, is faith-discourse and therefore polysemous in character. For these reasons religiosidad popular can be considered a locus of divine revelation.

REVELATORY ELEMENTS IN RELIGIOSIDAD POPULAR

Of the several culturally constitutive elements of Hispanic devotional piety, three of the most characteristic and, in my judgment, the most important, are tradition, a sense of history, and symbolism. Thése are the revelatory elements of religiosidad popular.

Tradition

Traditions are very important to a people. They are the collective memories of positive and negative experiences that have significantly affected their ongoing understanding of themselves. We have seen above how a tradition in TANAK is revelatory. We shall now see how traditions of religiosidad popular can be revelatory.

In religiosidad popular there is both a *traditio* and a *traditum*, a process and a content and an interaction between the two. The content of the traditions can be the specific devotions of a community, for example, the patronal feasts of a village and memories of what the patron saint has done or not done for the community. The process of the traditions can be the goal implementation of the specific devotion: the recitation of certain prayers or the performance of a definite task as part of the devotion, such as a pilgrimage to a specific shrine. The content and process are complementary as two parts of the one tradition.

In addition, the context of the tradition is important for its understanding, particularly its geographic context. Quite often a certain devotion is bound to a specific locale, giving that place an aura of sacrality, and the traditions connected with a sacral locus usually assume paradigmatic status within religiosidad popular. A prime example of this is the shrine of Our Lady of Guadalupe in Mexico City. Virtually all devotion to Our Lady of Guadalupe in the United States and Mexico has the shrine of Mexico as its prime referent.[33] All Hispanic traditions (memory experiences) concerning Our Lady of Guadalupe are somehow related to that shrine. The recipient of the Marian vision, the Indian Juan Diego, becomes the prototype for the Mexican—or devotee, usually mestizo poor—seeking special favor from Our Lady of Guadalupe. The place of vision was Mount Tepeyac. In both TANAK and the ancient Near East, the mountain was considered sacred space, the place of encounter between the transcendent and the human. Moses had his encounter with Yahweh on Mount Sinai. Also, the *tilma*, the shawl of Juan Diego where the Virgin Mary is believed to have left her imprint as a result of the encounter on Mount Tepeyac, is given a reverence that is equalled only by the shroud of Turin, where Jesus is believed to have left his imprint from the encounter with the divine on Mount Calvary.

The revelatory dimension in religiosidad popular's traditions is the interaction between memory and reinterpretation motivated by faith. A community may undergo significant positive or negative experiences—a bountiful harvest, flood, epidemic, and so forth. The experiences have an impact on the community, and the memory of these events preserves their meaning for the community. A case in point is the celebration of the feast of San Ysidro (May 15), patron saint of tillage in farming communities. The particular ritual includes a procession into the fields with the image of the saint where the priest in the name of the community and through the intercession of San Ysidro blesses the fields, either in gratitude for a successful harvest or in further petition in case of unsuccessful harvest. The harvest may be a success or a failure; reasons are found to explain, understand, and accept either result. These results, together with their reasons, are given an interpretation that becomes part of the community tradition. The memory of the harvest's outcome is interpreted as revelatory of God's will in the sense that the community's interpretation of the outcome (success or failure) is a faith-filled reinterpretation that has particular meaning for this specific community at this exact moment in history. This interpretation is expressed in ritual for subsequent retelling and reinterpretation in the tradition. The important thing in the ritual is to ask for the intercession of San Ysidro as someone who has special intercessory influence with God.

In a faith community, these events are given a religious meaning that is determined by the nature of the relationship with God. The challenge becomes one of fathoming God's will in such a meaningful event. The event may have one meaning for one generation and another meaning for a subsequent generation. What is significant here is to see the reinterpretation of memory in the context of the prayerful devotion as revelatory of

God's will. Each generation taps into the collective memory of the faith community, as represented by its religious traditions, in order to see what "God's will" (revelation) was for a particular generation at a given time, and then reevaluates it for itself. The devotional practices of religiosidad popular allow for this process in the traditions in the sense that the tradition is basically the memory of a collective experience which, in its "passing on," incorporates the dynamic of self-involvement so there is something of each generation in subsequent interpretations of the tradition. In other words, "God's will" (revelation) has as its nucleus the primary interpretation of the experience, which is evaluated and appropriated accordingly by later generations. This is how revelation occurs in the traditions of religiosidad popular.

History

Revelation through history, as noted earlier, has its limits as a comprehensive view of revelation. Nonetheless, it presents us with a legitimate way of seeing a manifestation of the divine will in human events. A very necessary part of the revelation-through-history approach is the interpretation of the events themselves. We have seen how in the Jericho story of Joshua 6, revelation through history was not in the facticity of the events but in their interpretation. The interpretation of the Jericho story was an integral part of Israel's traditions and memory regarding God's saving activity on her behalf. Religiosidad popular has a similar sense of history in that what predominates is not so much the facticity of events as their interpretation. In religiosidad popular, history and its revelatory impact have meaning to the extent that history's significance is interpreted by and for each generation.

One example of this dynamic would be "miracles" that are experienced as a result of "visionary experiences," usually of the Blessed Virgin. The multiplicity of Marian apparitions among devotees of devotional piety[34] suggests a need to recognize the feminine dimension of God—affective aspects such as tenderness and caring concern—in a world where the patriarchal values of power and domination are experienced as overwhelming. First, the "vision" is *believed* to have occurred, and this belief (interpretation) has its effect on the believers as indicated by the sudden surge of pilgrims to the locale of the "apparition" site. Second, it is of little or no importance to the believers that outsiders cannot prove the facticity of the visionary experience, but the effect of the belief, since it is believed to be from a heavenly source, is frequently interpreted in terms of a "miracle" such as a healing, which may have psychological or other natural explanations. The point is that God is revealing himself (his will) in the history of the believers because the believers are interpreting the revelatory experience as having meaning for themselves.

Another example of this revelation-in-history approach through interpretation could be a community's devotion to Our Lady of Guadalupe in light of the concrete historical experience of oppression, say as happened with the farm workers in Delano, California, in the early 1970s. One segment of the community experiencing powerlessness in the face of powerful growers interprets the message of Guadalupe as one of acceptance of the status quo in hopes of a better future—a sort of messianic expectation. Meanwhile, another segment of the community in the context of historical oppression interprets the meaning of Guadalupe in a more active sense, to the point of placing her banner at the head of protest marches.

Symbol

Revelation through symbol in religiosidad popular is basically two-dimensional: that which takes place through the symbolism in the various devotional practices and that which takes place through the Spanish language. I will follow Dulles' definition and understanding of symbol: "symbol is a sign pregnant with a plenitude of meaning which is evoked rather than explicitly stated." The key words here are *plenitude of meaning* and *evoked*.

Symbolism in the Devotional Practices. Every devotional practice in religiosidad popular has a certain amount of symbolism: significant event, gesture, object, place, and the like. And it is these symbols that have a revelatory dimension. Dulles mentions four properties common to symbolism and revelation that, in my judgment, are applicable to the symbolism in the devotional practices of religiosidad popular.[35]

Symbolism gives participatory knowledge that is self-involving. That is to say, the symbol speaks to us only insofar as it draws us into its world of meaning. In the devotional practices of religiosidad popular, this would mean that the specific symbol, such as the pilgrimage or home altar, becomes revelatory to the extent that the individual is drawn into the world of that specific symbolism, for example, pilgrimage as sacred journey, home altar as sacred space.

Symbol, insofar as it involves the knower as a person, has a transforming effect. The very "drawing into" the world of the symbol effects a certain transformation in the participant. Dulles mentions the healing capacity of symbolism as a fundamental effect.[36] In the devotional practices of religiosidad popular, this would mean that once drawn into the symbolic world of a specific practice, the participant has no choice but to respond, and the response itself becomes the transforming element. This transforming effect is usually a deepening of faith or a religious conversion, or could be one of several other possibilities. Often when there is some sort of "exchange" in the devotion, such as a cure for a penitential pilgrimage, the transformation is more obvious.

Symbolism has a powerful influence on commitments and behavior, stirring the imagination and releasing heretofore untapped resources of energy. Significantly, almost every social movement in history has galvanized its adherents behind some meaningful symbol. In the devotional practices of religiosidad popular, this would mean that whatever symbols were invoked in a specific devotion, the participant's involvement in and response to the symbolic world would result in some action. In the devotion known as the *manda*, a promise is made, generally to some saint, in thanksgiving or in exchange for a special favor—usually physical healing. The promise is often a pilgrimage to a sacred place, frequently symbolizing a return to mother earth. This journey is generally undergone with some hardship. A dominant symbol in this devotion would be promise as pact, a sort of quid pro quo. The granting of the favor would necessitate a strict obligation on the part of the participant to complete the promise of pilgrimage. The response here is expected because of the nature of the symbol. However, there are symbols in some devotions which are not bound to responses that are predetermined, but can allow for creative responses.

Symbol introduces us into realms of awareness not normally accessible to discursive thought. Because symbolism inhabits a world beyond empirical verification, it can put us in touch with deeper realities, such as the realm of the transcendent. In the devotional practices of religiosidad popular, this would mean nothing more than that the symbols of a particular devotion, because of their evocative and participatory aspects, bring the devotee into a world where faith and mystery are the common modes of discourse.

Symbolism through Language. Here we speak of Spanish as language in the context of religiosidad popular, which gives it privileged status because it is the language of worship.[37] It is only in its connection with religiosidad popular as religious communication in cult that Spanish as language can be considered revelatory. It would seem that any language can be considered to have revelatory potential when it speaks cultically, thus serving as a vehicle of communication between the human and the divine.

The hermeneutical work of Severino Croatto is instructive with regard to the revelatory aspect of language.[38] To use Spanish as an example, following established literary theory, we can posit a distinction between "language" (*lengua, idioma*) and "speech" (*hablar*). Language is generally considered a system of signs and laws regulating grammar and syntax based on structure and usually fixed. The activation of this system of signs is the task of "speech," which is normally referred to as the "event" of language. In the context of religiosidad popular, language would be the Spanish language *per se*, and speech would be the function of the Spanish language in the particular devotion itself, usually as prayer. The act of speaking circumscribes the meaning in the language. Croatto speaks of three factors that close off meaning in the act of speech: the sender who selects words to transmit; the message, the receiver to whom the message is addressed and who is able to decipher the message; and the context or horizon of understanding common to sender and receiver.

According to Croatto, language is potentially polysemous. It is the speech act that gives closure to this potential polysemy so there can be some sort of communication. In religiosidad popular, this means that Spanish spoken in the context of a specific devotion gives closure because it gives particular meaning within the symbolic ambience of the devotion itself. The sender, receiver, and context interact with one another to give *this* meaning to *this* situation within the framework of *this* devotion. And it is thus in the framework of symbolic interaction between language and speech as part of the specific devotion of religiosidad popular that revelation can take place as interpreted by the speaker.

SUMMARY AND CONCLUSION

One important aspect of revelation as faith-discourse in religiosidad popular has to do with its presumed appropriateness as revelatory discourse at this point in history, much as prophecy was during the monarchical period in Israel and wisdom and apocalyptic were in the postexilic period of Israel's history. We could offer two reflections.

First, there is the need of the times. During the time of the monarchy in Israel's history, when there was a dramatic sociopolitical shift in government from tribal federation to monarchy, there was a concomitant shift from concern for the poor and oppressed of society, as mandated by the Sinai covenant, to a lack of that concern fostered by unfettered consumerism. The Sinai covenant, which mandated responsibility to God and neighbor and proclaimed justice to all, was ignored, so the times called for a specific remedy. That remedy was prophecy. Prophets emerged to meet that need, and their primary message to restore responsibility and proclaim justice was enshrined in their writings. In our day and age there seems to be a great lack of precisely those values that religiosidad popular can offer, as cataloged by Puebla (454).

Second, there is the appropriateness of response. Because of its nature, prophecy in Israel was the most appropriate response to the abuses of the monarchy. *Prophet* means "one who speaks on behalf of someone." The prophets spoke with authority on behalf of Yahweh in order to restore covenant responsibility. This speaking by the prophets was a needed, direct confrontational challenge, which was the most appropriate way for communicating God's will at that time in that place to those people. Similarly, there is an appropriateness about the devotions of religiosidad popular since they express significant experiences of the Hispanic people in a language (symbolism) and a manner (affirmation of culture) that can be truly revelatory. The person-oriented, symbolic, intuitive, sensitive dimensions of religiosidad popular are most appropriate to counteract the cool, calculating, rigid, verbose, highly structured approach to relationship with God that seems to be common today in many churches.

This chapter has attempted to deal with the issue of revelation as a category by which to understand religiosidad popular in its relationship with the Bible by focusing on the nature and function of revelation as biblical category and on religiosidad popular as a locus of divine revelation. The nature of revelation was limited to those expressions where analogy between revelation in the Bible and religiosidad popular was deemed most effective: tradition, history, and symbol. Biblical traditions are seen as revelatory because of the interaction between memory and reinterpretation of the historical experiences that eventually become tradition. The salvation history presented in Israel's narrative is seen as revelatory more in the interpretation of the events rather than in their facticity. Symbolism in the Bible is revelatory because it involves the participant, influences his or her values, and has a transforming effect.

Religiosidad popular is itself a locus of divine revelation. The traditions, history, and symbols—including the Spanish language—constitute the nature of the specific devotions of religiosidad popular and are considered revelatory for much the same reasons as are tradition, history, and symbol in TANAK. Tradition in religiosidad popular is revelatory because of the interaction between historical memory and reinterpretation of a particular event enshrined in the celebration of a given devotion, and is remembered—and reinterpreted—in its retelling. The sense of history in religiosidad popular, as in TANAK, can be considered revelatory more because of what is believed to have happened than in what actually happened. Symbolism in religiosidad popular is revelatory because of its involvement of the participant, influence on the participant's values, and transformation of the participant. In sum, revelation in religiosidad popular occurs in its cultural constituents of tradition, history, and symbol.[39]

In order to avoid the impression that revelation in religiosidad popular may have superseded foundational revelation in the cosmic struggle between what some may consider the authoritative versus nonauthoritative in revelation, let me hasten to say that this is far from the reality. There is no supersedence. Rather there is complementarity, as we have seen in the discussion of foundational and dependent revelation. What my argument has tried to bring out in relief is the need for dialogue between the official church through her magisterium (albeit conditioned culturally and historically) and religiosidad popular as a different historical and cultural expression of divine revelation. Dialogue is the bridge of understanding and linkage between the two. It must begin by mutual recognition of strengths and limits and continues by mutual acceptance of the other's competency. By means of this process there can truly be a fuller and more complete understanding of God's revelation to humanity throughout history and among various cultures.

Before we begin with the biblical analysis of the four devotional practices it will be helpful to review and summarize the relationship between the Bible and religiosidad popular. First, there is the given relationship between the two for reasons mentioned in chapter 2. There is also the analogy between the two in the revelatory process discussed in this chapter. Finally, this relationship is further strengthened by use of the method to be employed in the subsequent chapters on devotional practices. First we shall seek biblical analogues with the specific devotional practice, grounding the analogue from the viewpoint of the biblical text through aspects of the historical-critical method. Then we shall attempt to strengthen the analogues from the viewpoint of religiosidad popular, using insights from cultural anthropology, current biblical hermeneutical methods, and insights from language theory. Finally we shall suggest pastoral implications through which Hispanic devotional piety can be better understood, appreciated, and applied to both liturgy and catechetics.

The first step in the method, that of seeking biblical analogues with the devotional practice using aspects of the historical-critical method, will present the viewpoint of the text. Only those aspects of the historical-critical method that are appropriate will be dealt with.

The second step in the method has three stages. The first stage involves insights from cultural anthropology. With respect to the four devotional practices for analysis, we have the given of a cultural relativism: God takes people where they are and deals with them in the context of the three levels of abstraction. In the context of religiosidad popular, that means religiosidad popular is part of the universal abstraction of relating to the transcendent, is part of the general cultural abstraction of worship, and is manifested by the specific cultural abstraction inherent in the individual religious practice. Where applicable to the four practices, we will discuss insights from cultural anthropology regarding the individual and the group: the value reinforcement by the individual interacting with the group; perception of limited good, or the sense of powerlessness amidst competition and struggle and eventual reliance on horizontal relationships for affirmation, with the treatment of God and/or saints on personal terms as seen through the ritual of the specific practice; and kinship and marriage, primarily kinship as expressed through the sacramental system or other religious rites performed in church that provide further affirmation.

The second stage involves insights from recent biblical hermeneutical theory, namely structuralism and reader-response criticism. Structuralism deals with the affective dimension of interpretation and asks how the historical text can affect the reader. There is the deep structure of narrative in the biblical text, which is common to all people and allows for identification of the reader with the elements of the narrative. There is also the deep structure of myth, the paradigmatic world of symbolism that allows the reader to identify with mythic universals such as the struggle between good and evil. The recent biblical hermeneutical theory of reader-response criticism also sees the reader as prime interpreter of the biblical text. What is essentially communicated by the text to the reader is a series of attitudes and feelings, made possible by the semantic universe of the biblical text applicable in the reader's context. There is also in reader-response criticism the bipolar reality of biblical text and reader who must interact before there can be meaning. The third stage will take into account insights from language theory where deemed useful or necessary.

Finally, the third step in the method provides pastoral implications suggested by the previous steps. This pastoral orientation shifts the concerns of religiosidad popular from a world of theory into a world of practice, with hopes that in this concrete fashion a deeper understanding and appreciation of religiosidad popular may result. Beyond the understanding and appreciation of religiosidad popular, the pastoral agent should become sensitized to the potential of Hispanic devotional piety for developing genuine spirituality and theology.

To achieve this, familiarity with the biblical material will be essential. It is difficult, if not impossible, to know with exact certitude how Hispanic practitioners of devotional piety interpret the biblical material apart from the personal experience of the pastoral agent. Thus the aim of the following chapters that deal with specific devotions is to provide the pastoral agent with some tools for making explicit some implicit assumptions that devotees of religiosidad popular have with regard to the Bible, and to affirm those insights. Preliminary pastoral suggestions pertinent to the specific devotion will be offered in each chapter, and an overall pastoral plan will be suggested in the final chapter. It is, above all, the biblical connection of these devotional practices that forms the basis for positing Hispanic devotional piety as a basis for an indigenous North American theology.

4

Ash Wednesday

EXPLANATION OF THE DEVOTION

One of the most widespread of Hispanic devotional practices in the Southwest is the celebration of Ash Wednesday. In the church's liturgical cycle, Ash Wednesday holds a prominent position as the beginning of the penitential season of Lent, reaching a crescendo in the sacred Triduum of Holy Week (that is, Holy Thursday, Good Friday, and Holy Saturday) and culminating in the joyous announcement of the resurrection of Jesus Christ at the Easter Vigil. Ash Wednesday is a focal point of liturgical commemoration for the Christian, one the church rightly emphasizes, for its penitential dimension, as appropriate to remind us of our mortality and the values of penitential practice, such as fast, abstinence, and good works.

The Ash Wednesday service generally consists of the celebrant blessing the ashes, normally made from the burning of palms from Palm Sunday, and distributing them to the faithful by tracing with the ashes a sign of the cross on the forehead. The accompanying prayer reminds the faithful of human mortality or of one's baptismal commitment to the Gospel. This rite of ashes is usually, though not always, connected with the celebration of the Eucharist which connection provides the broader liturgical framework for the significance of the ashes.

A source of constant frustration for many pastoral agents during Ash Wednesday services has been and continues to be the annual phenomenon of long lines waiting to receive the ashes. The ceremony of ashes is usually accompanied by a liturgy of the Word or the celebration of the Eucharist. In the context of Eucharist, the lines for ashes are frequently many times longer than those waiting to receive communion. This phenomenon has provoked the question as to why many Hispanics will make a heroic effort to receive ashes on the forehead on this day and think nothing of missing Mass on Sunday, a day of obligation, or of neglecting other sacraments. On the scale of official church values, the Mass—with its sacrament of the Eucharist—is the source and center of Catholic life and definitely much more important than the reception of ashes, which is but a sacramental. But yet, the phenomenon persists. Our biblical analysis according to the method proposed will offer some insights into this phenomenon.

BIBLICAL ANALOGUES OF ASHES

The Hebrew word for ashes (*'ēfer*) occurs quite often in the TANAK with multiple symbolic references. Of these symbolic references, four have special interest for our study: ashes symbolizing punishment; ashes as symbol of mourning; ashes as symbol of penance, a humbling attitude, and suffering; and redemptive quality of ashes.

ASHES SYMBOLIZING PUNISHMENT

One biblical passage in particular symbolizes well a connection between ashes and punishment: Ezekiel 28:18. Ezekiel 28 is a lament over the king of Tyre. This chapter in Ezekiel is important for several reasons, not the least of which is the richness of its creation theology.[1] The lament proper, in verses 11–19, describes in graphic imagery the rise and fall of the mythical first man, a common motif in the ancient Near East. There are hints of this "first man" theology depicted in Ezek. 28 paralleled in Ps. 8; Prov. 8:22; and especially in Is. 14:12–14. Perhaps the strongest connection, albeit with major differences,[2] is with the Genesis account of *'ādām,* the "first man" (Gen. 1:26–27; Gen. 2–3). Both are punished after a fall from a pristine state. The punishment is very much connected with the land. In Genesis, 'ādām is punished through his relationship with the land, that is, the ground (*'adāmāh*) is cursed because of the sin of 'ādām (Gen. 3:17– 18). Perhaps the strongest reminder of the consequence of 'ādām's sin is his fate in relationship to 'adāmāh. "In the sweat of your face you shall eat bread till you return to the ground, for out of it you were taken; you are dust and to dust you shall return" (Gen. 3:19).[3] The return to dust (*'āfār*) is the ultimate punishment for 'ādām,[4] as it was for the royal figure of Ezek. 28:18. In the case of the Ezekiel figure, he is "cast to the ground for his sin" (Ezek. 28:17), consumed by the fire of judgment, and "turned to ashes ['ēfer] upon the earth" (Ezek. 28:18). Dust and ashes ('ēfer) are reminders of sin and punishment.

In this biblical text, we have ashes symbolizing punishment. The case of Ezekiel and the lament over the king of Tyre connects ashes as symbol of destruction and punishment with creation theology. The link is with the fate of the "first man." In the creation story of Genesis, the play on the words "man-ground" ('ādām-'adāmāh) shows the relationship first in blessing (Gen. 1:28–30) then in punishment (Gen. 3:17–19). The land, as a result of 'ādām's sin, is now a hostile entity. Similarly, the royal figure in Ezek. 28, as part of this "first man" theology (Ezek. 28:12–15) and as a result of his sin of pride, will be cast to the ground, which is now a hostile entity. The Hebrew is very specific. The royal figure will be consumed by the fire of judgment, and as result will be "turned to ashes ['ēfer] upon the earth ['erets]" (Ezek. 28:18).

ASHES AS SYMBOL OF MOURNING

The use of ashes to symbolize mourning often occurs in the combination phrase "sackcloth and ashes." Of the several possible examples to illustrate mourning as symbolized by ashes, I choose three: Esther 4:1, 3; 2 Sam. 13:19; and Is. 61:3. The book of Esther, ca. fifth century B.C.E., is generally considered to be a form of haggadic midrash, that is literature that amplifies fictionally an historical nucleus for edification or didactic purposes. In this case God delivers his people through the intercession of a woman. The book also deals with the origin of the feast of Purim—lots. In chapters 3–4, Mordechai learns of a plot to kill all Jews on a certain day, which is determined by lot. This plot was given expression in a letter sent from the king to all the provinces and soon became a cause for mourning, so Mordechai tears his clothes and puts on "sackcloth and ashes" (Esther 4:1). When the Jews in the provinces become aware of the king's decree, they also go about in mourning, as indicated by their fasting, weeping, wailing, and lying in "sackcloth and ashes" (Esther 4:3).

The example of mourning in the passage from 2 Sam. 13 recounts the rape of Tamar by her half-brother Amnon, as the result of a devious ploy. The story is told within the context of the "succession narrative" (2 Sam.–1 Kgs. 2), namely how Solomon became king even though he was not David's eldest son, traditionally the heir. After having been mercilessly ravished by Amnon and then thrown out of his presence, thus compounding the crime, Tamar mourns not only her present situation but also her future fate as well. She expresses this mourning by putting ashes ('ēfer) on her head, tearing the robe she wore, placing her hand on her head, and crying aloud as she went (2 Sam. 13:19).

The final example of ashes as mourning, Is. 61:3, shows an interesting variation on the theme. This verse is part of a section that is cited by Jesus and proclaimed by him as the paradigm of his public ministry (Lk. 4:16–21). Chapters 56–66 of the Book of Isaiah are called Trito-Isaiah and are attributed to a prophet of the latter part of the sixth century B.C.E. The nucleus of the work is chapters 60–62, a message of salvation spoken to the Jerusalem returnees from exile. The message proclaimed in Is. 61:1–3 is reminiscent of the servant songs of Deutero-Isaiah (Is. 42:1–4 and 49:1–6), wherein as part of a messianic focus, justice and deliverance are proclaimed to the downtrodden. The significance of Is. 61:1–3 is that in this messianic vision a transformation will occur, from a negative state to a positive one, especially from mourning to joy. The prophet is "to grant those who mourn in Zion—to give them a garland [pe'ēr] instead of ashes [ēfer] . . ." (Is. 61:3). In this verse the antithetic parallelism is clear. The ashes of mourning usually placed on the head will be replaced by a garland of joy, also placed on the head. The words for garland and ashes use the same three Hebrew consonants, namely *aleph, pe, resh,* arranged differently but in parallelism to convey this theological truth.

In these passages where ashes symbolize mourning, we notice two interesting things. First, there is the direct bodily contact with the ashes. In the three passages there is a progression. In Esther, the contact is with the entire body (4:3). In 2 Sam. the ashes are placed on the head (13:19). In Trito-Isaiah, the ashes of mourning placed on the head are replaced by a garland of joy. The placing of ashes on the head is an important part of symbolizing the mourning. Second, in the passage from Trito-Isaiah, the context is important for a sense of the theological traditions contained therein. The messianic vision of peace and justice to be effected by the Anointed One is directed to the afflicted, lowly, downtrodden. Jesus made this clear regarding his own mission as the Anointed One, not only by his appropriation of this text (Lk. 4:17–21), but also by his identification with this group of people in the famous judgment scene (Mat. 26:31–46). One sign of the arrival of the messianic era will be when the afflicted, lowly, and downtrodden have their crown of ashes, signifying mourning, turned into a crown of joy.

ASHES AS SYMBOL OF PENANCE/HUMBLING ATTITUDE/SUFFERING

A third symbolic use of ashes in TANAK is as penance, humbling attitude, suffering, and similar states of mind.

Penance

One symbolic use of ashes as penance appears in Is. 58:5. As we noted earlier, this chapter is part of the corpus of Trito-Isaiah, therefore of the postexilic period. The focal point of the first half of chapter 58 is the fast days instituted after the destruction of Jerusalem in 587 B.C.E. and how they came to be kept. Motivation became a major problem, since abuses in the fasting and other penitential practices occurred (58:3–4).

Is the penitential ritual, especially the spreading of "sackcloth and ashes," to be a mockery? Not likely. Rather, the ideal fast with its ritual (58:6–8), showing striking similarity to Is. 61:1–3, has as its motivation what appears to be a liberation manifesto, namely loosening the bonds of wickedness, freeing the oppressed, sharing bread with the hungry, bringing the homeless poor into one's house, and clothing the naked. This is apparently an activist agenda that gives fasting—and any other penitential action—meaning because of the motivational element of righteousness.[5]

This penitential action of fasting and ritual with "sackcloth and ashes" (58:5), performed in conjunction with the acts of justice and compassion enumerated in 58:6–7, is a guarantee of Yahweh's presence (58:9). This passage from Trito-Isaiah focuses clearly on the role of ashes as part of penitential ritual, namely that it must be clearly bound to the *doing* of justice, and offers specific examples in that regard.

Humbling Attitude

Of the several possible citations where ashes can symbolize a humbling attitude or a self-effacing modesty, the text of Daniel 9:3 proves quite helpful. In addition to being midrash, the book of Daniel belongs to the postexilic literary genre known as apocalyptic, where the author's message was often hidden in symbolic language. Major reasons for the rise of apocalyptic literature were the historical tension and threats to religion and culture being experienced by the Israelites. Apocalyptic literature was a way by which the people were able to cope.[6] The historical context for Daniel is the spread of Hellenism and the threat of persecution by Antiochus Epiphanes in the second century B.C.E. Chapter 9 turns out to be a commentary on Jer. 25:11–14, which makes it a *pesher,* a midrashic commentary on prophetic writings. The threat of the end time mentioned by Jeremiah is reinterpreted by Daniel into a prayer of confession and repentance, part of which includes the humbling attitude of turning one's face to the Lord, ". . . seeking him by prayer and supplication with fasting and sackcloth and ashes ['ēfer]" (Dan. 9:3).[7]

The threat of persecution was a concrete historical reality for the Jews of the postexilic period. In the face of this threat the author of Daniel turns to God, pleading in earnest prayer for an understanding of the passage in Jeremiah which speaks of the destruction of Israel's enemy. To merit this revelation, he disposes himself for understanding and acceptance with the humbling attitude of prayer, fasting, sackcloth, and ashes.

Suffering

Significant citations for ashes symbolizing suffering come from the Book of Job, namely 2:8; 30:19; and 42:6. The Book of Job is one of the premier works of the genre known as wisdom literature, which posits human experience rather than salvation history as the locus of divine revelation. Job was written in the early postexilic period principally to deal with the question, "Why do the innocent suffer?" and to challenge the prevailing notion of retribution, namely that misfortune is a punishment from God. Dealing with suffering is the central focus of the book.

Chapter 2 forms part of the prologue, in which Job is put to the test. After the announcement of four successive catastrophes to his family and property, Job refuses to curse God. The Satan, who is the principal adversary among the "sons of God," then challenges Yahweh to allow a personal evil to befall Job, to see how he would then react. A physical sickness is inflicted on Job, who then laments the fact by scraping himself of the sickness with a potsherd while sitting among the ashes (2:8).[8]

Chapter 30 is part of Job's soliloquy (chapters 29–31), which comes across as a complaint. He decries the ridicule received from his so-called friends and graphically describes the nature of his present sufferings, which culminate in his being cast into the mire and having become "... like dust and ashes" (30:19).

There appears to be a sense of progression in the symbolic use of ashes. Whereas in 2:8 and 30:19 ashes are connected with suffering, in 42:6 they symbolize repentance for having challenged Yahweh's role in the experience of suffering. Chapter 42 is the last part of the dialogical confrontation between Yahweh and Job (chapters 38:1–42:6), wherein Yahweh affirms his power over nature and creation and says Job has no business questioning Yahweh's motives for what Yahweh does. Job humbly submits to Yahweh's argument, admitting of divine power and his own insignificance by expressing a humbling attitude through repentance "... in dust and ashes" (42:6).

The intention of the Book of Job—how to deal with the problem of the innocent sufferer—bespeaks a universal experience. Other sapiential literature of the ancient Near East also dealt with the theme of the innocent sufferer.[9] In these passages cited above, Job first expresses his innocent suffering caused by the Satan through mourning in ashes (2:8). Then Job describes as part of his suffering the ridicule of his friends, which he compares to being cast into the mire and becoming like dust and ashes (30:19). In his dialogue with God, Job seeks reason for his suffering and is reminded of the inscrutability of divine motivation, and so is reduced to accepting the divine will—still not fully understood—through repentance of presumption by sitting in dust and ashes (42:6).

REDEMPTIVE QUALITY OF ASHES

Thus far we have seen ashes symbolizing punishment, mourning, penance, a humbling attitude, and suffering. However, there is a tradition in TANAK that sees ashes as having a redemptive quality. This tradition is found in Numbers 19 with a distinct connection in the New Testament to Hebrews 9:13–14.

In the Book of Numbers, the Israelites, wandering in the wilderness and on the verge of conquest, still find time to perform important cultic ritual. One of these important rituals is the purification rite described in chapter 19, where the ashes of the red heifer are mixed with water and used for purification (19:9). It is clear in verse 9 that the purpose of this ritual is "... for the removal of sin," and said ritual is elaborated in verses 17–19. The redemptive quality of water is seen in the traditions of the Exodus motif—crossing the Reed Sea—and the Flood story, where the chosen people are saved and their enemies are punished through the instrumentality of water. However, water in the desert takes on a more significant and obvious life-giving quality, which is enhanced in the ritual by being mixed with the ashes of sacrifice.

A later example of the redemptive quality of ashes is seen in the New Testament Letter to the Hebrews, where direct relationship is established between the redemptive value of the water and ashes in Numbers 19 and the redemptive value of the blood of Jesus Christ.

> For if the sprinkling of defiled persons with the blood of goats and bulls and with the ashes of a heifer sanctifies for the purification of the flesh, how much more shall the blood of Christ, who through the eternal spirit offered himself without blemish to God, purify your conscience from dead works to serve the living God (Heb. 9:13–14).

This passage in Numbers 19 represents a tradition of the redemptive quality of ashes when connected with cultic ritual. This tradition of redemption through ashes was reinterpreted in New Testament times through the Letter to the Hebrews, which makes direct reference to the ritual in Numbers 19 and connects it with the ritual sacrifice of Christ on the cross. We have, thus, an example of the polyvalence—multiplicity of meanings—of biblical symbolism as seen in the symbolism of ashes from the above illustrations of destruction, punishment, mourning, penance, humbling attitude, suffering, and redemption.

ASHES IN RELIGIOSIDAD POPULAR REFLECTING ANALOGUES

Step one of our method has been to see ashes in the biblical text in terms of the text itself. Step two will see how the polyvalent symbolism of ashes in the biblical text can have its analogues in the Hispanic devotional practice of Ash Wednesday.

But first a summary of the previous section. The polyvalent symbolism of ashes in the TANAK has shown us the following:

First, in the text where ashes symbolize punishment (Ezek. 28:19), we saw a connection between ashes and the land. In Ezek. 28:18 the royal/first man figure was part of creation theology, which includes reference to the 'ādām-'adāmāh, "man-ground" pairing, as well as humanity in its pristine state of right relationship to God. This figure will be cast to the ground and turned into ashes in punishment for sin.

In the texts where ashes symbolize mourning (Esther 4:1, 3; 2 Sam. 13:19; Is. 61:3), there is direct bodily contact with ashes. The placing of ashes on the head symbolizes mourning. There is a reminder that the ashes of mourning placed on the head of the lowly, afflicted, and downtrodden will be turned into a garland of joy—likewise placed on the head—in the messianic era.

In the texts where ashes symbolize penance (Is. 58:5), humbling attitude (Dan. 9:3), and suffering (Job 2:8; 30:19; 42:6) we see, first of all, that for ashes to be part of a true penitential ritual, they must be linked with the *doing* of justice. Ashes symbolizing a humbling attitude are a necessary predisposition to understanding and accepting God's will. Ashes can also

symbolize suffering, experienced on different fronts, but when confronting
God it is necessary to accept his will.

In the text where ashes have a redemptive quality (Num. 19:9), they take
on their redemptive quality as part of cultic ritual, as for example in the
New Testament when connected with the cultic ritual of Christ's suffering,
which was redemptive for humanity (Heb. 9:13–14).

As we develop part two of our method, we shall deal with three central
themes of the symbolism of ashes that can strengthen the biblical analogues
from the viewpoint of religiosidad popular. These three areas are: connection with the land; ceremony of ashes on the forehead; and relationship
with God through the devotion.

CONNECTION WITH THE LAND

For Hispanics, as for the Israelites of TANAK, relationship with the
land was and is basic for identity. Hispanics have a close relationship to
the land not only because of a need for a sense of belonging to a land that
is their own but also because of their great respect for the beauty and
elemental forces of nature. This relationship of respect for nature, especially the land, has profound roots in the perception of the land as sacred
space, a notion, no doubt, obtained through close connections with a vestigial agriculturalism. It is in the seasons of seedtime and harvest that God's
creative energies are re-released and experienced. Earth is one of the four
basic elements—along with air, fire, and water—most of antiquity believed
constituted the life forces of the created world. Death was believed by many
ancients to be a return to the womb of mother earth. It is this concept that
underlies the biblical 'ādām-'adāmāh parallelism of Gen. 3:17–19 and the
fate of the royal figure in Ezekiel 18:18.

On the very pragmatic level of a special relationship to a land that is
one's own, we note that before the Treaty of Guadalupe Hidalgo in 1848,
which ceded most of the Southwest to the United States, the land belonged
to Mexico. There are those who still claim that the land was stolen. For
the Hispanic of the Southwest, any loss of land, for whatever reason—be
it the treaty of Guadalupe Hidalgo, the defrauding of private property by
entrepreneurial Anglos (which has been the case in northern New Mexico),
or any personal deprivation of land and the inability to retrieve it or receive
adequate compensation—is an experience of powerlessness. This fact of
powerlessness, which is a rupturing of a special bond between the Hispanic
and the land, is experienced as psychological and spiritual chaos. It is in
this connection that the Ash Wednesday service can serve as a framework
for healing.

In the Yahwist account of creation (Gen. 2:4b–24) the 'ādām-'adāmāh
linkage is quite strong. In Gen. 2:5 part of the reason given for the existence
of chaos is the not-yet-realized relationship between 'ādām (humanity) and
'adāmāh (ground/land). Then in verse 6b the ground ('adāmāh) is fertilized,

and in verse 7 the Lord God forms humanity ('ādām) from the ground/land ('adāmāh) thus establishing the eternal link between the two. Gen 2:7 becomes a key verse in this symbiotic relationship. "Then the Lord God formed man [hā'ādām] of dust ['āfār] from the ground [hā'adāmāh] and breathed into his nostrils the breath of life; and man became a living being" (RSV). The words "the man of dust" (hā 'ādām 'āfār) are in genitival apposition, indicating the nature of 'ādām before Yahweh's life breath was imparted. Like a potter the Lord gives shape to 'ādām, who is of dust/clay ('āfār), from 'adāmāh, and then breathes life into the creature. Thus in the Yahwist account of creation dust, ground/land, and humanity are inextricably linked.

In Gen. 2:9 all trees, including the tree of judgment for 'ādām, come from 'adāmāh. In verse 19 all good things for 'ādām are provided by God through the instrumentality of 'adāmāh, thus strengthening the bond of harmony between the two. However, because of 'ādām's sin in Gen. 3, part of the punishment meted was the now-disordered relationship between 'ādām and 'adāmāh. The Lord God says to 'ādām ". . . cursed is the ground [hā 'adāmāh] because of you. . . ." (Gen. 3:17), listing the extent of the curse (verse 18) and reminding 'ādām that you will return to 'adāmāh from whence you were taken. ". . . for you are dust ['āfār], and to dust you shall return" (Gen. 3:19, RSV). The disordered relationship is one of constantly seeking control of one by the other. The disordered dominance by 'ādām is manifested in the exploitation and pollution of 'adāmāh. The dominance of 'adāmāh is noted by the fact of 'ādām's return to 'adāmāh for burial after death.

The Ezekiel passage under consideration (Ezek. 28:17–18) shows the influence of the Yahwist creation account in Genesis, especially with regard to the 'ādām-'adāmāh connection. However, in Ezekiel the royal figure is spoken to in direct address and his relationship is to 'erets, which also means "ground." Because of his sins, the royal figure is cast to the ground (verse 17). "To be struck or thrown to the ground is an expression meaning defeat."[10]

We note a distinct parallelism between Gen. 2:7, Gen. 3:19 (both Yahwist passages), and Ezek. 28:17–18.

1. In Gen. 2:7 'ādām-'āfār ("man of dust") is formed from 'adāmāh. There is a creative and life-affirming relationship between the two.

2. In Gen. 3:19 we note that as punishment for sin, 'ādām is to return to the ground ('adāmāh) from which s/he came. "You are dust ['āfār], and to dust ['āfār] you shall return." Thus we see that in these passages 'āfār (dust) and 'adāmāh (ground) are connected with 'ādām's blessing and punishment.

3. In Ezek. 28:17, because of his sin, the royal figure (analogue to 'ādām) is cast to the ground ('erets/'adāmāh).

4. In Ezek. 28:18, the royal figure is "turned to ashes ['ēfer] upon the earth ['erets]," thus solidifying the symbiotic relationship between the two.

In these three passages we note the parallelism between ashes ('ēfer) and dust ('āfār). With respect to 'ādām, the creative, life-giving element of dust ('āfār) in Gen. 2:7 becomes the sign of punishment in Gen. 3:19, which punishment is echoed in Ezek. 28:18 through the substitute parallelism of ashes ('ēfer).

For the Hispanic, the ashes on Ash Wednesday can be a reminder of the strong bond that exists with the land: of the life-giving relationship through creation and harvest and of the adversarial aspect of the relationship because of sin. As basically an agricultural people, the Hispanics have more than a passing relationship with the land, which relationship is deepened religiously through the ceremony of ashes.

CEREMONY OF ASHES ON THE FOREHEAD

There are two key biblical passages dealing with ashes on the head: 2 Sam. 13:19, where ashes are placed on the head as sign of mourning and Is. 61:3, where ashes on the head as sign of mourning are changed to a garland on the head as a sign of joy in the messianic era.

In the Ash Wednesday ceremony, with its ultimate focus on the Resurrection—Easter as the key to the messianic age—the ashes are placed on the forehead (head), and can symbolize mourning, self-abasement, humility, and a reminder that mourning will be turned into joy. It will be left to the pastoral agent to bring out the specific meaning based on the particular Hispanic's personal experience. J. G. Plöger states:

> Like dust (Josh. 7:6; Ezek. 27:30; Lam. 2:10; cf. Job 2:12; 16:15) and ashes (2 S. 13:19; Est. 4:1), 'adāmāh was sprinkled on the head (Is. 4:12; 2 S. 1:2; 15:32; Neh. 9:1) as a sign of mourning, self-abasement, and humility. The original apotropaic (protection from demons by disfigurement) and magical (union with the lot of the dead) rite is adopted, preserved, and at the same time eliminated in traditional usage. It could remind the Israelite of his own nothingness (dust and ashes) (Gen. 2:7; 3:19; 18:27; Sir. 10:9; Is. 26:19; Job 20:11; 21:26; Ps. 22:30[29]), and be a sign of humble submission to divine providence[11] (italics mine).

RELATIONSHIP WITH GOD THROUGH THE DEVOTION

The biblical passages dealing with ashes that can promote a special relationship with God are those that present ashes as a predisposition to accepting God's will (Dan. 9:3); as a sign of repentance (Job 42:6); and whose use to be effective as penitence must be coupled with the doing of justice (Is. 58:5). These attitudes are constitutive of the Sinai covenant relationship between Yahweh and his people, where personal responsibility predominates. The significant relationship between Yahweh and his people is further expressed in the symbolism of ashes as having a redemptive quality when part of a cultic ritual (Num. 19:9). This redemptive aspect of ashes is appropriated by the New Testament in reference to Jesus (Heb. 9:13–14).

For Hispanics, the ceremony of Ash Wednesday can bring out the special relationship that exists between themselves and God if they can see the ashes as symbolizing a disposition to doing God's will, a repentance effectively achieved when coupled with the doing of justice, and a promise of redemption. Again, it would be the task of the pastoral agent to help surface these meanings based on the Hispanic's personal experience. Memory and tradition can be the reserve from which that interpretation surfaces.

INSIGHTS FROM ANTHROPOLOGY AND HERMENEUTICS

The principal insight from cultural anthropology appears to be the perception of the limited good, specifically as it relates to the use of ashes as symbolizing penitence for rivalries and jealousies within the community. Effective penitence is coupled with the doing of justice, which means the right ordering of relationships with others. The right ordering of the relationships might include a disposition to accept God's will, which could eventually result in realizing the ultimately redemptive aspect of what the ashes symbolize, namely salvation.

Recent biblical hermeneutical theory offers structuralism and reader-response criticism to help us understand the meaning of ashes for Hispanics. Both methodologies purport to underscore the *affective* dimension of biblical interpretation, that is, involving the reader or hearer in the process of understanding. In structuralism, there is the deep structure of the narrative, with its affective dimension. In the biblical texts where there is direct contact between the ashes and the body or head (Est. 4:1, 3; 2 Sam. 13–19; Is. 61:3), the devotee of religiosidad popular, who is affective by nature, is able to identify with the emotion of lamentation or mourning in the texts for any suffering experienced when the ashes are placed on the forehead during the Ash Wednesday service. There is the added feeling of hope that the ashes of suffering or mourning placed on the forehead symbolize a future joy—when the particular wound is healed.

Structuralism also has the deep structure of myth, the paradigmatic world of symbol that allows the reader to identify with mythic universals, namely, good and evil. This permits the reader of Is. 58:5 to connect the true penitential ritual of the reception of ashes with the doing of good deeds, especially the doing of justice. This is God's requirement in order to have a right relationship with him.

Reader-response criticism sees the reader/hearer as the principal interpreter of the text through attitudes and feelings that are communicated and the semantic universe of the text that is applicable to the reader/hearer's context through the interaction between reader/hearer and text.

The devotee of religiosidad popular, when reading or hearing the texts in Job (2:8; 30:19; 42:6), is able to share Job's feelings of powerlessness through similar suffering, and may feel tried by God or other outside agents without understanding why. The ceremony of ashes may be a context where the individual confronting God by asking the why of a particular suffering (especially if not deserved) can accept the inevitability of God's will with an attitude of humbling acceptance. A further hope for the devotee is that the ashes have redemptive value through their connection with the redemptive sacrifice of Jesus, which is the Mass. This may be a way to cope with the inexplicability of suffering. By participating in the liturgy of Ash Wednesday, the practitioner of religiosidad popular can see the liturgy itself as a pledge toward redemption at Easter by being reminded that as the ashes of the heifer were mixed with water (Num. 19:9) to effect redemption, so the ashes of Ash Wednesday have their redemptive significance by reminding us of the saving waters of Baptism more expressly identified in the rite of the Easter Vigil.

REVELATORY ASPECT OF ASH WEDNESDAY

In chapter 3 the notion of religiosidad popular as a locus of divine revelation was established. The basic cultural elements of religiosidad popular are tradition, a sense of history, and symbol.

The interaction between memory and reinterpretation of an historical experience that eventually becomes tradition can be revelatory. In the case of Ash Wednesday, an experiential relationship with one of the biblical analogues for ashes would first have to be established, then its interpretative memory would give it the force of a tradition that would be revelatory. History is revelatory more in the interpretation of events, the effect they have on people, rather than in their facticity. In the case of Ash Wednesday, the revelatory aspect of history would consist in how the individual interprets the biblical analogue as having direct, effective, personal meaning. Symbol is revelatory because it involves the participant, influences values, and has a transforming effect. In the case of Ash Wednesday, the symbolism of ashes is revelatory to the extent that the devotee or participant is drawn into the world of the ashes' symbolism, influenced, and transformed.

To illustrate the above revelatory process in the context of Ash Wednesday, we can use the example of a Hispanic family of religiosidad popular devotees that experiences an event resulting in mourning. During a gangwar shoot-out near the family's house, the grandmother (*abuelita*) of the family is accidentally killed. This abuelita was the person who held the family together, so her loss is deeply mourned. Her death is remembered and retold at subsequent family gatherings, and at each retelling someone remembers something significant about abuelita, especially her virtues and how she personally touched the lives of everyone in the family. This collective memory and periodic retelling become family tradition.

At the Ash Wednesday service, as the family receives ashes on the fore-head and is reminded of mortality and service to the Gospel, it can be reminded of mourning for abuelita, and of the marvelous transformative things she did for different members of the family. She was present at the birth of each of my grandchildren to be of service, and as the children were growing up, she gave of her meager pension to buy school supplies, and so forth. The memory of these acts of generosity is recalled by each family member insofar as he or she was personally affected. This is historical remembrance. The memory of her untimely demise, spurred by the Ash Wednesday ceremony, recalls to the family the need for a quality life because of the unexpectedness of death. These memories provoked by the symbolic ceremony of ashes can then motivate the family members to per-form similar deeds of kindness through awareness of mortality and the need for a quality life. The context of understanding the meaning of abuelita's good deeds can become revelatory for each family member to the extent that he or she remembers a specific act and finds it personally applicable. This is symbolic involvement.

PASTORAL IMPLICATIONS

This step is really more the concretizing of the method rather than part of the method itself, so the implications that will be suggested are more for their pastoral effect than for anything else. I would offer three general areas of concern for the pastoral agent.

ACCEPTANCE

As mentioned earlier, the pastoral experience of Hispanic participation at an Ash Wednesday service can be both overwhelming and frustrating. The challenge of acceptance is the internal disposition that tells the pastoral agent, first of all, that there is not only value but theological validity in the Hispanic culture and great personal worth of the people. This means under-standing the cultural values as expressed in the Hispanics' devotions, including Ash Wednesday, and not rushing to judgment without first attempting this understanding, acceptance, and appreciation.

PEDAGOGY

The challenge of pedagogy is the challenge of communication. How is the pastoral agent to communicate to others the positive values of Ash Wednesday—as suggested in general terms by Puebla and specifically by the foregoing discussion—in light of the negative elements the pastoral agent may encounter? The pastoral agent will have to evaluate both the context of the practice and the means available for positive pedagogy and then proceed accordingly. One suggestion is that the pastoral agent take

into account not only the flexibility of the contemporary biblical-herme-
neutical approaches of structuralism and reader-response criticism, but also
remind the practitioner of devotional piety of the historical-critical method
promoted in the traditional church teaching on ashes as a sacramental and
link the Ash Wednesday devotion to Easter, thereby promoting the values
of correct penitential practice as tied in with the doing of justice and awareness of the redemptive dimension of ashes.

ADVOCACY

The pastoral agent who has accepted the value and theological validity
of Hispanic culture and communicated the positive values of ashes must
now promote to the hierarchical church and nonunderstanding pastors the
richness of the devotion by pointing out the potentialities for spiritual
growth. That all this must be done in spite of ecclesiastical bureaucratic
obstacles will provide a formidable challenge indeed, and should not be a
cause for discouragement. This kind of advocacy is a matter of justice.

As one who functions in both camps, the pastoral agent is the prime
promoter of dialogue between the church and religiosidad popular. This
promotional approach of advocacy has the effect of incarnating the redemptive message of Jesus in the world through the appreciation and understanding of the culture of a people.

5

The Quinceañera

EXPLANATION OF THE DEVOTION

Virtually every society has its rites of passage from one age to another.[1] Anthropologically speaking, one of the most significant of these rites is the passage from childhood to puberty, for with this rite of passage the community or tribe publicly acknowledges a young person's acceptance of responsibility, which will somehow benefit the community. In the case of a young man, the community has a new "warrior" to protect and provide for its needs. In the case of a young woman, the community has a potential "mother" to nurture and strengthen it by providing for its continuity. It is the anthropological situation of the young woman that is of concern here.

At its most basic, all religious ritual has anthropological roots.[2] The *Quinceañera* celebration in the Hispanic culture, though overtly a religious ritual, is based on the anthropological reality of a young woman's capacity for motherhood. Quinceañera refers to the special fifteenth birthday celebration of a young woman, which, in Hispanic culture, is the fixed point in the young lady's life when the capacity for motherhood is publicly recognized in a religious and secular context—the Mass and the fiesta. This anthropological datum of a young woman's readiness for motherhood is the human reality underlying the Quinceañera celebration. Therefore, two key anthropological notions for religious consideration are fertility and right order.

Fertility is the basic potential context for life. It is being in rhythm with the universe as a creative life force that is generative throughout history, thus giving an aura of immortality. For many agricultural societies the creative force in nature was the most dominant, which is why often the chief deities in the pantheon of these societies were earth, sun, water— and all those elements where life was actively or passively generated. Fertility was frequently connected with woman, as is further evidenced in ancient societal rituals such as the *hieros gamos*, sacred prostitution, and other similar practices. Fertility was a way of acknowledging and celebrating the continuity of life—especially for a community. Most Hispanics of the Southwest have roots in an agricultural society and so possess great reverence for woman and her fertility.[3] One stage of reverence in the Hispanic framework is the time of puberty, which begins the young woman's capacity for motherhood, and this is what is celebrated in the Hispanic custom of the Quinceañera.

Right order means having a right relationship with the sacred in order to offset the negative influence of chaos. It is the nature of ritual to provide religious meaning for simple events. Ritual lifts the simple event of puberty into the realm of the sacred by putting it in elementally transcendent terms, such as the primal struggle between good and evil, which is more biblically described as the struggle between creation—representing the powers of goodness and life—and chaos—representing the powers of darkness and evil. Cultic ritual is the constant attempt to maintain creation victorious over chaos.[4]

On a basic level, the creative forces symbolized by a young woman's fertility are celebrated by the community as an affirmation of its own potential for continuity. The ritual context enables the young woman's life potential to take on transcendent status.[5] The ritual celebration of her fertile status ensures a right relationship with the creative forces of the cosmos and thus a victory over chaos, not only for the young woman herself but also for the community. So the ritual must be taken seriously.

Unlike the Ash Wednesday service, which is an already established ritual in the universal church that Hispanic devotional piety re-appropriates for deeper understanding, the Quinceañera religious celebration is the church's accommodation to Hispanic culture and devotional piety.

Though there is no universally fixed ritual for the Quinceañera celebration in church, the basic pattern is virtually the same whatever ritual is used. The young woman renews her baptismal promises and makes a public commitment to be of service. A common and very useful ritual is that published by the Archdiocese of Guadalajara, Mexico.[6] There is a severe paucity of material on the Quinceañera, and what is generally available is more of the descriptive how-to style than an in-depth analysis of the theological dimensions of the devotion. The popular work of Sr. Angela Erevia, a Missionary Catechist of Divine Providence, is of this descriptive nature.[7] For our purposes, I will use the ritual from Guadalajara as the basis for my analysis. The rite of celebration normally takes place during the celebration of Mass, between the liturgy of the Word and the liturgy of the Eucharist, usually after the homily.

In its pastoral introduction to the celebration, the Guadalajara ritual emphasizes strongly the evangelizing aspect of the celebration with regard to both the young woman and the community that shares in the celebration. The pastoral focus is on the girl's acceptance of the responsibility to be of service to the community—the family, the parish, and ideally a broader-based group. Thus the renewal of the baptismal promises and the commitment to be of service to the community can be considered the central elements of the Quinceañera ceremony.

In the rite of the Quinceañera celebration, several significant steps occur. First the minister reminds the young woman of the baptismal promises made on her behalf by her parents and godparents, the profession of faith, and commitment to live a Christian life. Now that she is considered a responsible person capable of assuming consequences for her own decisions—the capacity for motherhood allows that assumption—the minister, in the name of the community and in the presence of her parents and godparents, asks the young woman to renew those promises on her own. She then makes a public profession of faith and public commitment to be of service to her community as fulfillment of the earlier promise to live a Christian life. Then there is the blessing of a gift, usually a Bible, rosary, or a prayerbook, which symbolizes the rededication.

In these four parts of the ritual we notice some biblical underpinnings. In the first part, we see the ritual function of "memory": the young woman is asked to reaffirm the significance of the baptismal promises made on her behalf the day of her baptism. This is reminiscent of the cultic *Vergegenwärtigung* phenomenon we have seen earlier.[8] The young woman, as a recognizably committed Christian, is then asked to renew her original commitment by a church representative. This is reminiscent of the rededication rituals of the Sinai covenant that Israel, through Mosaic mediation, made to assure herself of continued covenant protection (see especially Deut. 5:1–5; Deut. 30:15–20; and Joshua 24). Then the young woman makes her public profession of faith and commitment to "serve the Lord," as was the case with Israel (implicit in the citations above from Deuteronomy and explicit in Joshua 24). Blessing of the symbol of rededication is reminiscent of the ratification of covenant which in TANAK is either a ritual meal or a sacrifice. In the Quinceañera celebration during Mass, it is fitting that this final part of the ceremony is followed by the liturgy of the Eucharist, which has festive continuity in the fiesta later celebrated by the family.

Thus we see that in the Quinceañera ritual, the two things that are centers of attention are the young woman's capacity for motherhood and her public recommitment to live her life as a Christian by dedicating herself to some form of service to a community. Both elements presuppose responsibility—one based on anthropological reality and the other based on religious (theological) reality.

BIBLICAL ANALOGUES TO THE QUINCEAÑERA

Since the central issues of the Quinceañera celebration are capacity for motherhood and public recommitment to live out the promises made at Baptism, and both require a sense of responsibility, it is fitting that our biblical analogues touch upon these two elements. Thus I have chosen the "young woman" of Isaiah 7:14 as the analogue for responsible motherhood and Joshua 24 as the analogue for the public recommitment.

THE YOUNG WOMAN OF ISAIAH 7:14

This particular passage falls within the framework of the Isaianic corpus known as the Book of Immanuel, chapters 7–12. In the latter third of the eighth century B.C.E., Ahaz, king of Judah and heir to the Davidic promises, is threatened by the kings of Damascus and Israel for his refusal to join the coalition against Assyria, the mighty empire of the period (2 Kgs. 16). Isaiah is told by Yahweh to go and speak to King Ahaz and give him encouragement in face of this danger. Isaiah goes with his son Shear-Yashub and, in the name of Yahweh, proclaims to Ahaz a hopeful sign that will assure divine protection of the Davidic royal house from its enemies. That sign of hope is the sign of the "young woman" and Immanuel in 7:14, which reads: "Therefore, the Lord himself will give you this sign: the young woman will bear a son and shall name him Immanuel."

First, the question of sign. In Hebrew the word for sign is 'oth, an omen, a symbol, something that points to a deeper reality. The fact that Isaiah's children had symbolic names has profound theological implications in the sense that the name of each child signifies a notable event in the history of God's people. Isaiah is told by Yahweh to go with his son Shear-Yashub to meet Ahaz (7:3). The name Shear-Yashub means "a remnant shall return," indicating that the name of the child will serve as a sign of hope for Judah. The name of the second son is Maher-shalal-hash-baz, which means "quick spoils; speedy plunder" (8:3). The symbolic name of the child here means that Assyria will carry out her threat of conquest.

Second, the sign of Immanuel. There are few passages in TANAK that have generated as much discussion as Is. 7:14. The varied opinions concern not only the meaning of the "young woman" but also the significance of the sign of Immanuel.[9] The sign of Immanuel is, above all, a theological theme with roots in Israel's long-standing belief in the presence of God among his people. The name Immanuel means "God with us." In the first five books of the Bible—Torah/Pentateuch—we note a tension between two viewpoints regarding God's presence among his people. One theological perspective views God as transcendent; that is, God is in his heaven and relates to humanity through a mediator. The biblical symbol in TANAK for this view is the Tent of Meeting. The other theological perspective sees God as immanent; that is, God is among his people and dwells in their midst. The biblical symbol in TANAK for this theological view is the Ark of the Covenant.[10] These two views represent an ongoing struggle within Israel to understand and relate personally to God's relationship with his people. The theme of Immanuel as presented in Isaiah moves the question of God's presence among his people to a new stage.

The Isaianic view of Immanuel seems to favor the perspective of immanence in the relationship between God and his people, and adds specificity to the Immanuel sign. That is to say, not only is the symbolic name interpreted in the text itself, but clues to his identity are given. At the end of verse 8 in chapter 8, the symbolic name of Immanuel is mentioned as a sign of hope in the face of the waters of judgment, and that hope is given credibility by the interpretation of the name of Immanuel at the end of verse 10.[11]

Who is to be the sign of Immanuel? Again, there are varied opinions. From the literary context, it is apparent that Immanuel was to have messianic qualities and would promote justice and righteousness as indicated in chapters 9 to 11. But above all, Immanuel would manifest in his life the implications of the symbolic name, namely what it means to recognize and accept God's presence in our midst. The symbolic aspect and its ongoing reinterpretation is more important as a process than any specific identification of Immanuel, since the believing community appropriating the Immanuel symbol reinterprets the symbol's significance for itself.[12] However, in order to assess Immanuel's significance and identity, it is first necessary to discuss the 'almāh.

The "young woman" of Is. 7:14 is called 'almāh in the Hebrew text. The word means a young woman of marriageable age, supposedly, but not technically, a virgin. The technical name for virgin in Hebrew is bethûlāh. The 'almāh's identification has been a source of theological controversy virtually from the beginning. Presumably for the symbol to have had immediate significance, Isaiah's contemporaries had to have some idea of who the 'almāh was. Subsequent opinions have ventured to identify her. One opinion has her as the wife of Ahaz, thus making Hezekiah, son of Ahaz, Immanuel. Another view sees the 'almāh as the wife of Isaiah in light of Isaiah's children all having symbolic names (Is. 8:18). The traditional opinion of Christianity sees the 'almāh as Mary, the mother of Jesus.[13]

A more plausible interpretation of the "young woman" of Is. 7:14, and by implication the identity of Immanuel, would be to see the oracle of Is. 7:14 in broader terms. That is to say, the oracle of Is. 7:14 was a pledge of hope that would find fulfillment not at one specific moment in history, but throughout all of human history. The presence of God among his people is an ongoing promise of effective love and concern.[14] The messianic characteristics of Is. 9, 11 further underscore the effectiveness of God's presence among his people: Immanuel would be a bringer of peace and justice. Thus the promise of Immanuel in Is. 7:14 is God's pledge to be with his people through the instrumentality of the 'almāh, and the effectiveness of that presence would be manifested by Immanuel, a messianic figure who would promote justice. It is plausible that King Hezekiah, son of Ahaz, was the first incarnation of the Isaianic oracle of Immanuel, and it is even more plausible that the Gospel writers saw Jesus as the final and definitive incarnation of Immanuel, a bringer of peace and justice. The 'almāh, then, was the young woman who, through her creative powers of motherhood and by her responsible cooperation, was and is the one to help bring about fulfillment of the Immanuel oracle, namely God's effective presence among his people. In a truly theological sense, God's promise of Immanuel could not be fulfilled without the responsible active affirmation and participation of the 'almāh.

THE COVENANT RENEWAL CEREMONY OF JOSHUA 24:1–28

The second biblical analogue helpful for understanding the Quinceañera ceremony, particularly the theme of commitment to the faith community, is the covenant renewal ceremony of Joshua 24.

In the TANAK there are basically two principal covenant traditions, though there are several covenants. The two covenant traditions are fundamentally in tension with each other, because they represent two antithetical ways of relating to Yahweh. Without excessive oversimplification, it can be said that one covenant tradition, the Sinaitic, described in Ex. 19–24, is characterized as being bilateral and conditional. It is bilateral in that it is between Yahweh and the Israelite people, and both parties are mutually obligated. It is conditional in that a choice is offered to the people: *If* they keep Yahweh's commandments, *then* Yahweh will be their God, with all that implies. The second covenant tradition, the Davidic, described in 2 Sam. 7, is characterized primarily as unilateral and unconditional. It is unilateral in that Yahweh binds only himself in the covenant with David. It is unconditional in that there are no specific stipulations for David.

Our focus of attention is the Sinai covenant tradition, which has as one of its constitutive elements conditionality, a sense of responsibility and commitment when a choice is made. To help illustrate the notion of commitment to service within the faith community as part of the Sinai covenant tradition, it is helpful to discuss Josh. 24:1–28.[15] Because of its general considerations as a covenant renewal ceremony, general scholarship posits Josh. 8:30–35 as the cultic context of Josh. 24.[16]

The geographical locus for Josh. 24 is the sacred site of Shechem, famous as a patriarchal shrine. Shechem sits in a valley between mounts Ebal and Gerizim in central Palestine, and is universally identified as Tell-Balata in Nablus.[17] Due to its history as a patriarchal shrine, it serves as the place where Joshua gathers the tribes together, now that they have entered the promised land under Yahweh's guidance and protection, to reaffirm their dedication and commitment to Yahweh as his people, as was initially proclaimed at Sinai.

The Sinai covenant constituted the notion of Israel as God's special people, as stated in Ex. 19:3–6. The mutuality of obligation reinforced by conditionality placed a certain priority on personal choice. The people were free to choose for or against the covenant. This was the basis of commitment. But to understand the commitment, some clarification of the covenant concept is necessary.

Much of scholarly opinion holds that the covenant model based on the Sinai tradition shows distinct parallels to the Hittite suzerainty treaty pattern, without attributing dependency of one on the other.[18] The significance of the parallelism lies in the weight given to the stipulations and the consequences, or, in other words, to the commitment and consequences of free choice.

The Hittite suzerainty treaty pattern generally has the following structure:

1. The preamble, where the suzerain identifies himself and his relationship to the vassal;

2. Historical prologue where the suzerain recounts the acts of benevolence performed on behalf of the vassal in order to motivate the keeping of the stipulations;

3. Stipulations, which are the treaty conditions set forth by the suzerain;

4. Reading the treaty in public reminds the vassal of the commitment made;

5. List of witnesses, usually nature deities, which are called upon to affirm what has transpired between the suzerain and the vassal;

6. Blessings and curses, which are the reminders of the positive and negative results of keeping or not keeping the treaty.

An apparent example of the Hittite suzerainty treaty pattern is Josh. 24, though not all of the above elements occur. For example, the preamble may be verse 2. The historical prologue is verses 3–13, and the stipulation is compressed into the simple command, "Serve the Lord." Provisions for public reading are made in verses 25–26, and the list of witnesses given are the people themselves in verse 23 and the natural elements in verse 27. The blessings and curses are implied as consequences of choosing to serve or not serve in verses 16–20.

The central element in this ritual covenant ceremony is the public commitment of renewal of the original Sinai covenant promises subsumed under the basic theme of "service." Verses 14–18 are the key verses for this notion of commitment through service. The word 'ābad, generally translated "to serve, work, toil, labor," occurs nine times in various ways. In these verses we get the idea that one group united around Joshua has made a decision for Yahweh, and the second group is presented with the opportunity of making the decision for or against Yahweh in this covenant renewal ceremony.[19] In verse 14 the people of the second group are told to serve Yahweh "in sincerity and faithfulness" and not the deities their ancestors had served in Mesopotamia and Egypt. This is first-level motivation by contrast. In verse 15 the language is reminiscent of the Sinai covenant formulation itself, with its conditionality and free-choice option. The people are asked to "choose this day for yourselves whom you will serve . . ."—Yahweh or other gods. At the end of verse 15 Joshua states that he and his group have already made the choice for Yahweh. In verses 16–18 the people enthusiastically respond to the challenge and choose to serve Yahweh because of all the wonderful things he has done for them—such as delivering them from slavery in Egypt—and will continue to do because of the covenant relationship. Thus in this covenant renewal ceremony there is the commitment to service as expressed in the original Sinai covenant, namely keep the commandments to love God and neighbor.

QUINCEAÑERA IN RELIGIOSIDAD POPULAR REFLECTING ANALOGUES

The *'almāh* of Is. 7:14, through her creative power of motherhood and by her cooperation, helps bring about fulfillment of the Immanuel oracle, namely God's effective presence among his people. Also, in the covenant renewal ceremony of Josh. 24 Israel makes a public commitment to serve Yahweh according to the terms of the original Sinai covenant, keeping the commandments to love God and neighbor. These two biblical analogues to the Quinceañera have been seen in terms of the biblical text itself. Now we shall attempt to strengthen these analogues from the viewpoint of religiosidad popular, supported by insights from cultural anthropology and recent biblical hermeneutical theory.

In the Quinceañera ceremony the Hispanic young woman of fifteen is certainly an 'almāh, a young woman of marriageable age. This capacity for motherhood is, from a cultural-anthropological perspective, a reality on the deep level of human universals: motherhood establishing relationship with transcendence on the issue of ability to generate life, that is the human mother and the creative God. In fact, Yahweh is sometimes presented in TANAK as having feminine as well as masculine characteristics, especially under the image of mother. In Jer. 31:20 the word for God's mercy and compassion is the same as for the female womb, *reḥem*. The image of God as mother is also clearly seen in Is. 49:15; Is. 42:14; Job 38:28–29; Deut. 32:18; and Num. 11:12.[20]

Also from the perspective of cultural anthropology, we see that in the Quinceañera ceremony, the young woman's public commitment to community service is, in effect, a bonding of relationship between herself and her support community—family, relatives, and friends. It is this community that, through the symbolism of the public renewal of her baptismal commitment, functions as her feedback group with regard to shared values. In addition, the kinship question has a certain prominence in the Quinceañera ceremony through the presence of the young woman's baptismal godparents, her *padrino* and *madrina*. The godparents usually have an active role in the ceremony, thus highlighting the importance of the kinship question. This active role, in addition to strengthening the level of kinship in the ceremony, can also express itself through economic assistance. There is a probable secondary level of kinship relationship established between the young woman and her *damas* and *chambelanes*—her female and male peers who accompany her to and from the altar as part of the entrance-and-exit ritual.

Concerning biblical hermeneutical methods and the Quinceañera, we can make the following observations. First, with regard to structuralism. If one of the readings for the Quinceañera ceremony or the preparatory classes includes the Is. 7:14 passage, then it is possible to confront the deep structure of narrative posed by the 'almāh and fulfillment of her role as mother of Immanuel. According to structuralism, the deep structure of narrative includes the disruption of order, the attempt to reestablish order with occasional hindrance, and the reestablishment of order. In the case of the 'almāh of Is. 7:14 and its surrounding passages, the disruption of the order could be Ahaz's refusal to accept a sign from Yahweh that he would be expected to receive. The attempt to reestablish the order could be Isaiah's oracle, which is the sign of the 'almāh and Immanuel. The reestablishment of order could be the expectation and eventual fulfillment of the 'almāh and Immanuel sign in the history of the Israelite people.

For the young woman at her Quinceañera, this would mean that her disruption of order could be reluctance or a possible refusal on her part to accept what God expects of her as a "potential mother" with responsibility: effecting the creative potential of making Jesus present in the community, or "birthing him" through her acts of service. The attempt to reestablish the order could be successful awareness of her responsibility as 'almāh in the context of the Immanuel oracle, that is effective fulfillment of making God present among his people once again. The reestablishment of order could be her acceptance of such a role in her life and the willingness to carry it out in the context of her community. As is often the case with Hispanic families (at least in my personal experience), there is usually some alienation experience from the church and religion. This dynamic of structuralism provides a useful evangelization tool during the period of instruction for the young woman and her family.

With regard to reader-response criticism, we see the reader or hearer as principal interpreter and the primary response as affective. The three postulates of reader-response criticism are: attitudes and feelings are what are communicated; the semantic universe of the text is applicable to the reader or hearer's context; and there is a bipolar reality of text and reader. They must interact in order for there to be meaning.

In the case of the covenant renewal ceremony of Joshua 24 and its relation to the Quinceañera ceremony, we make the following observations. The biblical passage, this or another, can be either a reading at the ceremony or part of the instructional preparation for the young woman and her family. If the young woman herself does the reading at Mass, she is a reader. If the biblical passage is read by another or is part of her instructional preparation, she is a hearer. In either case, reader-response criticism is applicable. Second, attitudes and feelings in the covenant renewal ceremony that could be communicated to the young woman are those of awe and wonder at the benevolent deeds God has performed in her personal history—granting the young woman health, a loving family, and so forth. Other feelings evoked could be those of gratitude, thus provoking motivation for the commitment renewal and a sense of trust in God's promises. Third, the semantic universe of the text is indeed applicable to the reader or hearer's context in that the symbolic world of the covenant renewal ceremony in Josh. 24 is wide open to interpretation in the young woman's personal context, for example implications of accepting or rejecting the choice for God. Fourth, there is the bipolar reality of the text and reader/hearer in that they must interact in order to have meaning. This is most clearly seen when the young woman publicly, as part of the ceremony, makes her own covenant renewal through the recitation of her baptismal renewal promises and proclamation of service to her community.

REVELATORY ASPECT OF THE QUINCEAÑERA

As an expression of religiosidad popular, the Quinceañera ceremony shares in its revelatory dimension. When we speak of religiosidad popular as revelatory we speak of tradition, a sense of history, and evocative symbolization of a specific devotion. We also speak of the polysemous quality of the faith-discourse in the devotion—communication of the meaning of the devotion to many generations. In the case of the Quinceañera, the revelatory traditions are those life experiences of the young woman. That is to say, there are bound to be some positive or negative life experiences that are significant for the young woman and her family. From a negative point of view, there could have been some grave childhood illness or death in the family that might have had an alienating effect. From a positive point of view, there might have been some special recognition received. These events represent key moments in the young woman's life that are remembered by her and her family. These are her traditions. The celebration of the Quinceañera, because of its religio-cultic orientation, becomes an occasion for these traditions to be remembered and responded to, for example, awareness of greater dependency on God and family for support and spiritual survival, or awareness of a greater sense of gratitude to God and family for blessings received. This interaction between memory and its interpretation in tradition can result in a revelatory experience.

The revelatory dimension of history—what is believed to have happened and its effect on the believers—lies more in its interpretation than its facticity. In the case of the Quinceañera ceremony, a sense of history would differ from tradition to the extent that the sense of history is a sense of the young woman's cumulative life experiences as part of a broader continuum, rather than a specific *traditio* or *traditum* as suggested above. In other words, a sense of history would be the young woman's sense of the meaning of her life. The occasion of the Quinceañera ceremony would be the threshold moment of the rite of passage, enabling her to evaluate her past life and its future directions in light of available options. The linkage provided by that evaluation in terms of what her life has meant and what it can mean, especially through the ritual of the covenant renewal ceremony, provides a revelatory moment.

For symbol to be revelatory, the interpreter must participate in the symbol's meaning—given the broad semantic field—be influenced by it, and experience a transformation. In the Quinceañera celebration the two chief biblical analogues are replete with symbolic potential to draw the young woman into participation and transformation. For example, the Isaianic oracle on responsible motherhood and Joshua's covenant renewal ceremony on commitment to service provide an ample framework for involvement and transformation. Responsibility and service to community are two important qualities evoked by the symbolism of the biblical analogues. They can evoke participation on the part of the young woman at the Quinceañera ceremony and, if the ceremony is taken seriously, will effect a transformation. In this sense the symbols of the Quinceañera ceremony (the biblical analogues) can be considered revelatory.

As to the faith-discourse of religiosidad popular, we see that its revelatory aspect generally lies in the community-wide interaction between memory of an originary event—significant experience—and its contemporary interpretative relevance. Each generation interprets the meaning of an event for itself. The revelatory dimension of this faith-discourse comes into being as the believing community speaks for itself the meaning of God's will, made apparent earlier in its history, now apparent in this contemporary context of a specific devotion.

In the case of the Quinceañera ceremony, the faith-discourse becomes revelatory when members of the faith-community of family, plus friends and parishioners, interpret as relevant for themselves the meaning of any life traditions of the young woman, her sense of personal cumulative history, or the symbols of the ceremony itself. The revelatory aspect may be made more evident, for example, if the young woman's public commitment to service is viewed by the faith-community as both relevant and transformative for the young woman.

PASTORAL IMPLICATIONS

Pastoral implications of the devotion of religiosidad popular assume great importance. They are the logical conclusions and practical extensions of our theological and biblical analysis of the specific practice of devotional piety. For the Quinceañera ceremony, I would offer three areas of concern for the pastoral agent.

ACCEPTANCE

There are still many places in the southwestern United States with heavy Hispanic populations where Hispanic parents would like to celebrate the

Quinceañera of their daughter, but find themselves at odds with their pastors, primarily because of misunderstandings about the nature and purpose of the Quinceañera. Rejection of a devotion that is culturally embedded in the consciousness of a people is perceived as rejection of the people themselves. Sensitivity to a people's culturally bound faith-expressions (especially when those faith-expressions seek the church's official blessing as the Quinceañera ceremony does) begins by acceptance of the people themselves, then of their faith-expressions. A logical concomitant of acceptance is understanding, which occurs only with dialogue. This dialogue with understanding is a fundamental responsibility of the pastoral agent.

PEDAGOGY

One of the principally effective pedagogical tools is dialogue between the pastoral agent and the practitioners of religiosidad popular, dialogue based on mutual respect and understanding. Some suggestions for fruitful dialogue would be: a series of instruction for the young woman, her parents, and her godparents regarding the significance of the Quinceañera and the sense of responsibility it presupposes; encouragement of reception of the sacraments; promotion of participation by parents and godparents in the ceremony—bringing up the gifts, blessing the young woman, writing the petitions, proclaiming one of the readings, and so forth. In effect, whatever would promote mutual understanding and appreciation between Hispanic culture and the hierarchical church would be of great pedagogical value.

ADVOCACY

A more assertive role on the part of the pastoral agent would be required here than that of mediator or ombudsman. In order to accomplish this, the pastoral agent needs to be transformed culturally. Hispanics realize that official Church recognition of many of their devotional practices comes very reluctantly, if at all. The pastoral agent is in an excellent position to point out to the official church the positive values and benefits of the Quinceañera ceremony. For example, the pastoral agent can point out to the young girl the tremendous witness value of her commitment to be of service to the community, and to the Hispanic family the cautionary aspect of the Quinceañera celebration, namely that the family not be lulled by the festive dimension completely and lose sight of the religious dimensions of the Quinceañera celebration.

6

The Home Altar

EXPLANATION OF THE DEVOTION

The Hispanic devotion of the home altar transports the devotee into the realm of sacred space. It is, above all, a sort of theophanic manifestation of the divine presence in one's home. Mircea Eliade states that the home, like the church, shares in sacred space. In both home and church, the threshold is of extreme importance, because it is the passageway between the sacred and the profane worlds. So the threshold has its guardians— spirits that protect the sacred space from profanation.[1] The altar in the Church is the focal point of sacredness, the space where the divine presence is manifested in ritual. So it is in the Hispanic household.

From a phenomenological point of view, the house shelters power which is distributed throughout the house. And in the house, the hearth, fireplace, or kitchen is the central place of power. The phenomenologist Gerhardus van der Leeuw puts it this way:

> The possibility of eating and drinking is experienced precisely as a divine possibility, and its position estimated as holy. This is also the basis of the sacredness of that most important spot of all in the house, the hearth: it is its central point, the totality of its power ... Even today the common people have preserved some of the correct feeling that the power of the house accumulates in the kitchen, on the hearth: the "best parlour" usually remains empty![2]

In fact, Webster's unabridged dictionary, second edition, gives as the second definition for hearth, "the fireside as the center of family life; the home; family circle."[3] Thus the kitchen is generally seen as sacred space, central to family activity.

It is interesting to note that in Hispanic homes, at least in the villages of northern New Mexico, the kitchen is indeed the most important room in the house. One enters a Hispanic home through the kitchen and visits in it. All visitors are received first in the kitchen, and then may or may not be ushered into another "parlor." This centrality of the kitchen in the Hispanic household reflects a vestigial awareness of the sense of the sacred in the home, which is why Hispanics consider hospitality a test of their closeness to God. All visitors to the Hispanic household are first offered some refreshment upon entering. Since the hearth/kitchen is the entryway into the Hispanic home, the focal point of the house as sacred space, the meal then seems to function as a sort of bonding ritual. In a certain sense, the hearth/kitchen becomes a kind of "altar" where, through the ritual of meal/hospitality, a kind of divine manifestation is experienced. A parallel is recognized by van der Leeuw: "House and temple, therefore, are one: both are the 'House of God.' Hearth and altar are also one, the temple-altar being the table and fire-place of the gods."[4]

However, in some Hispanic homes there is a more determinative and conscious attempt at localizing divine presence, the home altar. It is usually a simple affair, an altar set up in a nook in the family room or master bedroom. There is usually a predominant statue of Mary or Christ in one of their manifestations, frequently attended by other saints. More often than not there are flowers and votive candles on the altar.[5] The dynamics of encounter in the devotion take the form of prayer, usually of petition and/or thanksgiving. Favors are requested and gratitude is expressed for favors granted. The sense of sacred space and ritual activity is quite evident. Jesus, Mary, and the saints, in their various manifestations, generally express the primary concern of the practitioners: Mary in her pivotal role of mediatrix with God; Jesus in his human dimension, such as the Sacred Heart, symbolizing love and compassion; St. Jude as patron of the impossible; St. Anthony of Padua as patron of lost articles, and so forth. The overriding sense of the existence of the home altar is the manifestation of the divine presence in the home. God is there for his people.

This concept has serious implications vis-à-vis the official church. Since the divine power is believed to be accessible in the home, there is not a great need to seek mediatorship through the priest or official Church liturgy. Also, because of the sense of divine presence in the home through the home altar, there is a feeling of personal relationship to God, Mary, Jesus, and the saints, manifested not only in the forms of familiar address but also in the treatment of the statuary. Sometimes if a favor is not granted, the statue of the "offending" personage is turned toward the wall.

As a youth, I recall our family home altar dedicated to both the Sacred Heart and the Immaculate Conception. The altar was often decorated with the usual array of an occasional candle and flowers from our garden. Our family form of prayer was the daily rosary and a subsequent litany of prayers and what seemed like interminable petitions and acts of gratitude. There was no doubt in our minds that there existed a pervasive sense of divine presence during those ritual moments of prayer.

BIBLICAL ANALOGUES TO THE HOME ALTAR

Since the central concept of the Hispanic home altar is manifestation of the divine presence in one's home, one of the most suitable biblical analogues would be the theme in TANAK of God's presence among his people. In TANAK there are two principal theological traditions that deal with Yahweh's presence among his people, and both have political implications. One is the theological tradition of God's transcendence, symbolized principally by the Tent of Meeting. This implies structure and the need for mediation. The other is the theological tradition of immanence, symbolized principally by the Ark of the Covenant, and implies direct relationship with God. Because of their political implications, these two theological traditions have been in tension not only throughout Israel's history, but also throughout the history of those institutions, ancient or modern, that base their relationship to God on one or the other tradition.

THE TENT OF MEETING

The nature and origins of the Tent of Meeting are shrouded in obscurity. The Tent of Meeting tradition bears a strong connection with the theological tradition of Tabernacle, though it is not identical with it.[6] Prevailing opinion sees that the traceable origins of the Tent of Meeting and Tabernacle traditions come from the period of Israel's wanderings in the wilderness under the leadership of Moses,[7] and that the Tent of Meeting is but one manifestation of the Tabernacle as the symbol of Yahweh's presence among his people.

The first five books of the TANAK, also called the Pentateuch, are generally considered to be comprised of four major blocks of tradition: the Yahwist (J), dating from ca. ninth century B.C.E.; the Elohist (E), dating from ca. eighth century B.C.E.; the Deuteronomist (D), dating from ca. seventh to sixth century B.C.E.; the Priestly (P), dating from ca. sixth to fifth century B.C.E. Often these traditions, with their own characteristics, are intertwined in the Pentateuch, and at times become difficult to separate.[8] The two major tradition blocks dealing with the Ark and Tent are the epic (JE) and priestly (P), and it is the desert period (Israel's exodus to the conquest of Palestine) that is generally considered to be, chronologically, the theological origin of the Tent and Ark traditions. The desert period, Israel's formative stage as Yahweh's people, is described at length in the Pentateuch, specifically in the biblical books Exodus to Deuteronomy, and is thus a focal point for many Pentateuchal traditions.

One of the various names given to the Tabernacle (*mishkan*, "dwelling"), which is the major symbol of Yahweh's presence among his people, is the Tent of Meeting (*'ōhel mô'ēd*), found in both the epic and priestly traditions. The Tent of Meeting was primarily a place of revelation where Yahweh communicated to Moses, not a place of cult.[9] This place of revelation where Yahweh communicated principally with the mediator, Moses, had strong political implications in the sense that this theological perspective necessitated mediatorship for effecting divine presence. Passages reflecting this revelatory aspect of the Tent of Meeting are Ex. 29:42–43; 25:22; 30:36.

There is a definite theological connection between the covenant ratification at Sinai (Ex. 24) and the promise of Yahweh's presence with his people through a "dwelling place." The latter was to be a visible reminder of the mutual commitment expressed in the former (Ex. 19:5). In Ex. 25:8, strengthened and clarified in Ex. 29:45–46, Yahweh makes this connection by asking for the erection of a *miqdosh*, a "holy place," a "sanctuary" where he might dwell with his people. For "to dwell" the Hebrew uses the verb *shākan*, which means "to pitch one's tent,"[10] and the noun form *mishkān* is a typical priestly designation of the Tent-sanctuary. This priestly connection with the notion of Tent-sanctuary is important, because in the postexilic period the priestly class continued the dynastic concept of the monarchy through its appropriation of the Davidic royal theology in the sense that the priests became the new "repositors" of divine revelation and the official mediators of Yahweh's will for the people. The political implications of this newly appropriated mediatorship role are obvious.

As Frank Cross points out:

In the Priestly strata, the term *mishkan* applies to the one tent, the Mosaic sanctuary ... Thus in P, *skn* is used invariably and solely to specify the "tabernacling" of Yahweh — the earthly presence of Yahweh — for the purposes of revelation and atonement ...

The common word in the Priestly materials, and throughout the Old Testament, which means "dwell" or "inhabit" is *ysb*. P uses the term *ysb* whenever it wishes to speak of men "dwelling"; but never of Yahweh or any manifestation of Yahweh to Israel ... When Yahweh is said to "dwell" (*ysb*), the place of dwelling is never on earth, in the temple, or in the tabernacle, but in heaven alone ...

The Priestly writers were struggling with the problem of divine immanence and transcendence, in other words, the problem of the covenant-presence in the sanctuary. Israel's cosmic and omnipotent God could not be confined to an earthly sanctuary. Yet the supreme object and benefit of the covenant relationship — of Israel's election in the great events following the Exodus — was God's new "closeness" in the tabernacle. It seems clear that this old word *skn* has been taken as the technical theological term to express this paradox ... *Yahweh does not "dwell" on earth. Rather he "tabernacles" or settles impermanently as in the days of the portable, ever-conditional tent.*[11]

The tabernacle, manifested as Tent of Meeting,[12] represented Yahweh's transcendence, since in order for the meeting between Moses and Yahweh to occur in the Tent, Yahweh had to "come down" from his heaven into the Tent. A key passage dealing with this issue is Ex. 33:7–11. It belongs to the JE block of traditions, but is not a unity because of the discrepancies.[13] The entire chapter 33 has as thematic thread binding the presence of Yahweh among his people. The guarantee of the protective divine presence is connected with the Sinai covenant experience, because it was Yahweh personally through the theophany who covenanted himself mutually with the Israelite people. The Sinai event thus becomes paradigmatic. Though the covenanting is with the people, Moses is the necessary mediator. Once the people leave Sinai, the question becomes one of the continuity of God's presence with his covenanted people, and the Tent and the Ark become two principal symbols representing two differing theological traditions dealing with the question of Yahweh's ongoing presence, at times in conjunction and at times in competition.

Chapter 33 of Exodus is significant in this regard. In verses 1–3 Yahweh will not accompany his people because of their evil ways. He withholds his presence pending an act of repentance. The key verses in the chapter are verses 7–11, which, according to Brevard Childs, seem to be out of place since verses 12ff. continue with the idea of God's deprivation of his presence. The tent mentioned in verses 7–11 is undoubtedly the Tent of Meeting of the early JE traditions and not the tent of the Priestly writer described in Ex. 25–31.[14] It is pitched outside the camp to indicate that Yahweh is still withholding his full presence from the people but is communicating with them through a mediator, Moses. When the manifestation of the divine presence seemed opportune, the early desert tradition of God's presence in the pillar of cloud materialized. Yahweh descended in the form of the pillar of cloud to the entrance of the Tent and communicated himself to Moses. Thus we have here a transcendent God manifesting a presence to his people through the continuity of the Exodus symbol of the pillar of cloud, coming down to the Tent of Meeting outside the camp and revealing himself to Moses. Transcendence approximates immanence; the people know that Yahweh is present to them but are only able to know what Yahweh wants through mediatorship.

There is a patent parallelism between Ex. 33:7–11 and the Sinai theophany linking the keeping of the covenant with assurance of the divine presence. Yahweh manifests his saving presence as long as the covenant is kept by the people. In both the Sinai theophany (Ex. 19–24) and Exodus 33:7–11, the manifestation of God's presence takes place outside the camp, the people are kept at some distance, God descends in a pillar of cloud, and Moses speaks with God. The symbol of the cloud, especially as coming down, is a significant element in the theological notion of transcendence.[15] There is thus a strong link between the Tent of Meeting and God's presence as transcendent; he comes down from heaven for special communication to the people through Moses. Walther Eichrodt puts it this way: "As *'ōhel mô'ēd*, the Tent of Meeting, it seems as a place where Yahweh can meet with Moses ... It is, therefore, explicitly the transcendent God who here manifests himself and directly implies his envoy without the use of any machinery of mediation."[16]

THE ARK OF THE COVENANT

The second Israelite desert shrine to deal with God's presence among his people is found in the traditions of the Ark of the Covenant. As with the Tent of Meeting, there are some ambiguities concerning the nature and origins of the Ark. It was indeed an early Mosaic desert shrine, and some problem exists as to whether or not it was a part of the Tent tradition, since a later stratum of the tradition finds the Ark housed in the Tent, as in the case of David's political reorganization of the tribal federation at the time of the monarchy (2 Sam. 6–7).

Generally there are four perspectives from which to examine and study the Ark ('ārôn—"chest, box"). First, it is an extension or embodiment of the presence of Yahweh (Num. 10:35–36; 1 Sam. 6:3, 8, 20). Second, it is a portable symbol of God's protection during war in the premonarchic period (1 Sam. 4). Third, it is a container of the two tablets of the Decalogue—a sort of portable Sinai (Ex. 26:16, 21). Fourth, it is a portable throne for the invisible presence of Yahweh. Often these different strata of the Ark tradition overlap, so it is difficult to assign a specific date or place to each stratum. However, our focus of interest here is on the Ark as symbol of Yahweh's presence as expressed in the first two positions.

The earliest stratum of the Ark tradition is generally considered to be Numbers 10:35–36, the so-called Song of the Ark. In these verses the Ark is addressed directly, as if it were an extension of Yahweh's presence among his people. The plea for victory was specific because the hope for victory was strong. Through the Ark, Yahweh is addressed directly as a warrior (Ex. 15:3) who defeats his enemies, who also happen to be Israel's enemies. This notion of Yahweh as warrior is significant because historically Israel was frequently threatened by one or another military power. It was important for Israel's survival that she believe Yahweh was in her midst to defend her from all enemies, since it was uncertain when or from where an enemy would attack. This idea of the warrior-god takes on different forms[17] because it is very much part of Israel's understanding of God, such as the struggle with chaos as in creation (Genesis 1-2). For Israel, God's presence in her midst is a saving presence, a presence protecting from all harm. It is the presence of a victorious warrior. Walther Eichrodt says:

> The reason, therefore, why his [Yahweh's] might as a warrior is emphasized so strongly is not that he is regarded simply as a savage destroyer, but that this is the way in which the most impressive and immediately convincing demonstration of his rightful position as Israel's ruler [can be made known] ...

The sacred object of the Ark provided empirical support for this sense of having Yahweh in their midst; and the rites by which the war was sanctified also helped to concentrate men's thoughts on the presence of the God of battles. Hence the holy war belongs pre-eminently to the ages in which men were aware of being in an especially close relationship with the exalted God, and of experiencing his saving presence.[18]

Another element in the tradition of Yahweh as warrior-god reflected by the symbol of the Ark of the Covenant is seen in 1 Sam. 4–7.[19] Here Israel's defeat in battle by the Philistines is attributed to the lack of the Ark's presence in their midst (1 Sam. 4:3). Even though the Ark is brought back to be present in battle, not only is Israel defeated, but the Ark is captured by the Philistines (4:10–11).

How can this have happened? Yahweh has permitted his presence to leave his people as a form of alienation, because of the wickedness of the priestly house of Eli, as recorded in 1 Sam. 2. Verse 11 of chapter 4 mentions the death of Eli's two sons almost as a result of the Ark's capture.[20] Thus what we have is the alienation of God's presence from among his people because of covenant violations. That Yahweh is still in control is apparent from his victories while in exile: the Ark's destruction of the Philistine deity Dagon (5:1–5); affliction of the people of Ashdod with boils (5:6–7); and dissemination of panic among the inhabitants of Ekron (5:10–11). Finally, the Ark returns to Israel (chapter 6) and Yahweh is once again among his people, with the proviso that they repent and keep the covenant (7:2–9). As proof of the reestablishment of Yahweh's saving and victorious presence among his people, the Philistines are routed when they come again to attack Israel (7:10–11). This victory, together with the reestablished presence of Yahweh among his people, is commemorated cultically (7:12).[21]

POLITICAL IMPLICATIONS OF TENT AND ARK THEOLOGIES

It is a functional principle in TANAK that Israel's polity was a theocracy. There was an almost symbiotic relationship between theology and politics in the various traditions that explain the relationship between Yahweh and Israel. The theologies of divine transcendence and immanence reflected by the symbols of Tent of Meeting and Ark of the Covenant are a case in point. Since Yahweh's presence was effective power, whoever "controlled" Yahweh's presence had great power. Hence, any political legitimation of power must have some connection with the powerful and effective presence of Yahweh. Since transcendence and immanence as two forms of divine presence reflected two different political styles, there was a struggle within Israel for dominance of symbolism and, therefore, legitimation.

In order to understand the relationship between the Ark and the Tent traditions we must ask whether or not the Ark was always connected with the Tent from the beginning, since on occasion the Tent served as the repository for the Ark. Prevailing opinion generally assumes an independent origin of both, but with parallel development. Gerhard von Rad summarizes it thus: "We may regard the two conceptions of ark and tent as two currents flowing side by side in a single stream down the ages of Israel's religious history."[22]

I would say that the conjunction and disjunction of these parallel traditions were heavily dependent on political considerations, since God's presence supports a given political structure, monarchy, for example. As indicated earlier, one of the great values of symbol is its power to involve.

The final official conjunction of the two traditions takes place historically in the postexilic period, when the priestly writer places the Ark of the Covenant, the symbol of Yahweh's immanence, in the Holy of Holies of the Temple, the new Tent of Meeting that symbolizes Yahweh's transcendence. The idea of the priestly writer in the postexilic period, the time of TANAK's final editing, is to legitimate the priesthood as surrogate for the no-longer-existing monarchy. Therefore, the legitimating force of symbol — Ark in Tent — was put into play to gain general acceptance for the priesthood's political ascendancy. In the monarchic, exilic, and postexilic periods of Israel's history, the temple theology and all it implies was dominant. Consequently, the political aspects of the Ark and Tent traditions can be summarized in the following manner.

A key element in Israel's belief system is God's effective relationship with his people through his presence. Assurance of divine presence legitimizes the activities and decisions of those claiming that special presence. Is that presence direct and permanent, or is it mediated and occasional? Assurance of permanent presence among the people allowed for a special relationship between God and the people, a directness in the relationship that allowed for reciprocity in commitment and responsibility. There was a kind of "democratic" dimension to this type of relationship. For example, Yahweh related directly to all the people and all were directly responsible for keeping the covenant obligations. God's will in this instance was clear. On the other hand, mediated divine presence meant that a special person or group was the filter through whom God's presence (will) was made known to the people. There was a kind of "dynastic" dimension to this type of relationship, since only a kind of self-perpetuating elite, such as a monarchy or priesthood, could function as mediator of the divine presence.

The democratic and dynastic dimensions of relating to God, as political expressions, had their theological justification in the symbols and traditions that we find associated with the Ark of the Covenant and the Tent of Meeting. There have been and continue to be tensions and struggles for legitimacy and dominance between these two symbols in the minds of the people. For example, the Ark of the Covenant symbolizes a theology of "immanence," that is, God dwells among his people.[23] No mediator is needed to effect God's presence to his people. It is a direct and effective relationship. The covenant tradition that is most suitable to this kind of thinking is the Sinai covenant (Ex. 19–24), because it is both bilateral and conditional; it involves the people directly and consciously.

By contrast, the Tent of Meeting symbolizes a theology of "transcendence," that is, God comes down from his heaven, usually in a cloud, when communication with the people becomes necessary. A mediator is needed to effect the divine presence.[24] The covenant tradition that is most suitable to this kind of thinking is the Davidic covenant (2 Sam. 7), because it is unilateral and unconditional; it is made with an individual and his dynasty, and nothing is asked of the individual in return. This eventually became a carte blanche by which some of David's descendants felt themselves unaccountable to anyone.[25]

The contrasting but parallel Ark and Tent theologies vis-à-vis their approaches to Yahweh's presence provided a healthy tension in that it became clear there were legitimate options in relating to God. David's astutely political move when he became king of the disparate tribes was to combine the two competing symbols of God's legitimizing and effective presence, the Ark and the Tent, with the Tent/Temple theology as predominant (2 Sam. 6).[26] The political implications of democracy versus dynasty—as apparent in their symbolism and as expressed in contemporary church belief, discipline, and worship—make for a serious but interesting challenge to our theology and biblical interpretation. As it was for ancient Israel, so it is for modern Christianity: Politics and religion are more closely intertwined than most people care to admit. We can find these same tensions, together with their political implications, operative between the official church and the Hispanic practitioners of devotional piety, symbolized as they are by the Tent and Ark traditions respectively.

HOME ALTAR IN RELIGIOSIDAD POPULAR REFLECTING ANALOGUES

Of the two major theological traditions in TANAK dealing with God's presence among his people, transcendence—symbolized by the Tent of Meeting—and immanence—symbolized by the Ark of the Covenant—the one that best suits the Hispanic devotional practice of the home altar is that of immanence.

The TANAK theological tradition of immanence allows for God's direct and effective presence among his people. In the Hispanic home the home altar is the equivalent of the sacred shrine/holy mountain where God's presence is invoked. It is like a surrogate Sinai, where a covenantal relationship is established between God and his people, where there is a mutuality of responsibility and commitment. It is at the home altar where, on occasion, the pact or bargain is struck. This pact is an exchange. For a favor—usually healing—granted by God, often reinforced through the instrumentality of a favorite saint,[27] the petitioner will generally perform some penitential act. The direct mutuality of responsibility and commitment is effected at the home altar as it was on Sinai. Or, as is more often the case, the home altar as surrogate Sinai is the sacred meeting ground where a meaningful encounter between God and his people takes place through the ritual of prayer.

The theology of immanence in TANAK is connected with a warrior-god and the Ark. So in the devotional practice of the home altar a type of warrior-god is invoked. The Hispanic practitioner of the home altar devotion can sometimes feel oppressed or exploited in his or her proper environment, at work, or by society in general, and thus tends to seek relief from this oppression by appeal to a warrior-god who can assure solid victory from oppression. The oppression can take on different forms: illness in the family, exploitation in the marketplace, or any personal problem. Victory over this form of oppression (the chaos principle) becomes a prime concern for the petitioner, hence the binding nature of the pact made with the warrior-god at the home altar.

There are political implications with regard to the imaging of God's presence with his people. Tent theology (transcendence) promotes a human mediatorship, while Ark theology (immanence) advocates nonmediatorship through direct relational activity. The question is, who controls God's effective presence with the people, a human mediator or the people themselves? As we saw in chapter 1, the church was frequently in an adversarial relationship with Hispanics because she saw herself in the mediatorial role between God and his people. This was patent Tent theology (transcendence) in the sense that the official church functioned in the belief that God "came down from his heaven" and "spoke" to the official church mediators, who in turn communicated the divine will to the rest of the faithful, much as Moses did at the Tent of Meeting. By contrast, the Hispanic practitioner of the home altar devotion functions in the belief that God is directly accessible through the ritualized activity of the home altar, so there is no need for official church mediation.

An insight into the devotional practice of the home altar from cultural anthropology can be had through a modified application of the principle of perception of the limited good. A perduring sense of powerlessness in an Anglo-dominated society such as the United States, has left the Hispanic seeking self-affirmation through horizontal relationships on a peer level. Amid some acceptable competition for the limited physical and spiritual goods, the *compadres* in the community mutually assist one another to meet economic and social needs. The spiritual needs are met through communication with God and the saints on a peer level, quite likely through the home altar devotion. God and the saints are often referred to in familiar terms in the prayer surrounding the home altar devotion, and this familial context allows for a sense of affirmation on the part of the petitioner. The biblico-theological tradition that God is among and close to his people and deals with them directly, fits well the devotional practice of the home altar.

Also appropriate is Sinai covenant thinking, which promotes mutuality of obligation and accountability between God and the practitioner of the devotion—something compatible with the theory of perception of the limited good.

With regard to recent biblical hermeneutical theory and the home altar, both structuralism and reader-response criticism have something to offer. Structuralism permits an affective dimension in biblical interpretation. It seeks to determine how the text affects the reader. We have seen that this is generally accomplished through the deep structures of narrative and myth, characteristics common to all people.

We have posited a distinct link between the biblico-theological tradition of immanence and the devotional practice of the home altar. By applying the deep structure of narrative here, we see that in the TANAK story of the Ark of the Covenant there was disruption of order—removal of the Ark from the Israelite camp by the Philistines; attempt to reestablish order with occasional hindrance—the attempt to return the Ark; and eventual reestablishment of order—the eventual restoration of the Ark among the Israelites. This sequential narrative indicates the deeper reality of Yahweh affirming his presence, withdrawing his presence because of people's sin, and final reaffirmation of his effective presence.

In the devotion of the home altar, a similar deep structure narrative is functioning. By the very existence of the home altar and the ritual connected with it, the effective presence of God is presupposed, much like the theme of immanence in the Ark of the Covenant tradition. The petitionary aspect of the prayers, together with the *quid pro quo* element between God and the practitioner, presupposes a probable alienation of God's presence. This could be either the petitioner's feeling of unworthiness or alienation if the petition is not granted within a specified time. The effective presence of God is finally reestablished, either when the petition is granted or when the petitioner comes to accept the result.

Reader-response criticism likewise concerns itself with the affective dimension of biblical interpretation. Attitudes and feelings are what are communicated, and the semantic universe of the text permits applicability to the reader or hearer's environment. The biblical texts applicable to the home altar devotion are those connected with the Ark of the Covenant tradition and the theology of immanence. God's effective presence is experienced by the devotee, and this opens up a world of possibilities.

First there is the question of the biblical texts concerning the warrior-god. Hispanics in the United States have a long-standing history of oppression and exploitation from varying sources. This negative experience affects the psyche more than it does the body. Feelings of worthlessness and a generally poor self-image frequently leave the U.S. Hispanic in an extremely vulnerable condition. It is within this framework that the affective dimension of Scripture and its connection with religiosidad popular has its great appeal. Both structuralism and reader-response criticism as ways of understanding Scripture offer the Hispanic an opportunity for this much-needed sense of self-affirmation. The God who is effectively present in the home altar devotion will, as the warrior-god, confront and conquer definitively the devotee's enemy, be it illness, bad habits, exploitation, or any other manifestation of chaos. Attitudes of hope and expectation, coupled with feelings of confidence, anxiety, and love, are experienced in relationship to the warrior-god encountered in the home altar devotion.

There is also the question of attitudes and feelings connected with a covenant relationship. We have already seen that the most suitable covenant relationship model from Scripture applicable to the home altar devotion is the Sinai covenant relationship with its mutuality of responsibility and commitment. There are feelings of self-affirmation expressed in a relationship with a mutuality of responsibility and commitment. In addition, the theology of the Ark tradition, specifically with regard to the reading or hearing of the biblical texts, provides for an applicability in the devotee's environment within the framework of the home altar devotion. For example, when the practitioner reads or hears any of the biblical passages related to the Ark tradition within the context of the home altar devotion, the semantic world of the text's meanings is opened up so there can be applicability to personal life of any relevant part of the text. If such occurs, then there is an effective interaction between text and reader, the bipolar reality, and understanding takes place, which thus gives the biblical text meaning.[28]

REVELATORY ASPECT OF THE HOME ALTAR

As we have noted in our discussion of other practices, the revelatory dimension of a pious devotion is encountered in its traditions, sense of history, and symbols that the individual practitioners bring to and draw from the devotion itself.

We have seen earlier that the revelatory dimension in tradition is the interaction between memory and experience that is interpretation. It may well be that during the devotional experience of the home altar, the practitioner remembers a personally meaningful event, recent or remote, positive or negative, that has had a significant impact. The memory of this experience has undoubtedly been shared at one time or another with others in the family, and was given a value. That is to say, the experience was good or bad, depending on the criteria utilized for interpretation. In the context of the home altar devotion, the practitioner remembers an experience, recent or remote, that is most likely shared with the family. In the context of reflective prayer, the experience is given a value as either a good thing or a bad thing, with its implications. When shared with the family, this value-laden experience becomes a tradition, something that is handed down. When the implications are remembered and reinterpreted by different members of the family as well as by the practitioner, according to the value criteria shared earlier, revelation takes place.

Let us take the example of a Hispanic woman who in her youth married unwisely. Many years and several children later, her husband leaves her with the children and runs off with someone else. There is no doubt this is a source of trauma for the wife and her children. The event has had great significance and implications. This woman happens to have a home altar and is accustomed to bringing her problems there and dealing with them in ritual dialogue with God. This experience is tradition in the sense that her extended family has been very aware of her situation virtually since the beginning. There are those in the family who have ventured to make a value judgment, some saying she deserved what she got because she defied her mother, others saying she got a raw deal from her husband and is more to be pitied than blamed. During the devotional ritual in front of the home altar, the woman remembers the experience of the unwise marriage and its consequences. In her dialogue with God, examining the pros and cons of her action, she learns something about herself and the experience, and this process is revelatory. Family members engaged with her in the home altar devotion may also learn something from her experience for their personal lives, and thus the devotional experience becomes revelatory for them as well.

A sense of history takes on its revelatory dimension, as has often been said, through interpretation of the event rather than in its facticity. In the case of the home altar devotion, the practitioner brings positive and/or negative experiences of the family over a long period that have had special meaning. In terms of the effect these experiences have had on the practitioner or the practitioner's family, interpretations are made. If these interpretations are made within the context of the devotion, they can be considered revelatory, because God's effective presence in the home altar is a benevolent presence where communication is considered direct—that is, revelatory.

The home altar devotion can be considered revelatory with regard to its symbols, as well. The revelatory dimension of symbol lies in its involvement of the practitioner through the influence of values, and his or her transformation. If a direct connection between the home altar and the Ark of the Covenant biblical tradition were made and maintained, then the symbol-rich Ark tradition could speak directly to the practitioner of the home altar devotion. For example, the warrior-god concept of the Ark tradition presents the deity as victor over actual and threatened oppression and assures victory over chaos under whatever form, as long as there is an existing covenantal relationship between God and the practitioner. In the home altar devotion, the image of the warrior-god brings the devotee into the polysemous world of symbol, and whatever appropriation of the image speaks to the practitioner is to be considered a revelatory experience. A transformation takes place when the practitioner comes to realize the effective nature of appropriating the symbol; for example, liberation from oppression by the warrior-god demands reciprocity. In the case of the home

altar devotion, this could mean gratitude manifested in behavior or proclaiming the good deeds of the warrior-god. With regard to the home altar
devotion, it could also mean the warrior-god, as victor over chaos, comes
across more as an advocate or ombudsman in the manner of Boaz (Ruth
4:3) and the *gô'ēl* of Job 19:25.

When we speak of the revelatory context of a particular devotion, we
are speaking of the faith-discourse inherent in that devotion, which is basically: belief in the communication and understanding of specific meaning
provided by the dynamic of memory in traditions surrounding the devotions;
the interpretation of personal "history" surrounding celebration of the
devotion; or the transformative impact of the appropriated symbol from
the devotion. In the case of the home altar devotion, the revelatory context
would normally be consequences of the faith expressed in the overall
dynamics of the devotion. More simply put, because of the covenantal relationship extant through this effective presence of God in the home altar
devotion, God will keep his word as revealed through memory, history, and
symbol.

PASTORAL IMPLICATIONS

The pragmatic aspects of our study with respect to the home altar devotion are the pastoral implications of how that devotion is perceived by
pastoral agents and practiced by Hispanics.

ACCEPTANCE

The home altar devotion may or may not be a major issue in a given
parish, but it is generally popular in the Southwest. For this reason alone,
awareness of its existence and significance is necessary for a truly effective
pastoral agent. Traditional devotions in the Catholic church—novenas to
the Sacred Heart, Our Lady under various titles, and innumerable saints—
have conditioned pastoral agents to be accepting of people who find official
liturgical functions too abstract and sometimes remote. In addition, many
of our older churches have side altars and/or additional statuary to allow
for public expression of these devotions. If such allowances are made officially through the side altars and/or additional statuary in the Church
proper, then allowance should be made for devotions in the home, as exem-
plified by a home altar. In addition, pastoral agents visiting homes of the
elderly or the sick where there is a home altar can show respect by using
it for prayer or communion services.

PEDAGOGY

Once again, the pastoral agent is aided in evangelization through utilization of biblical material. Establishing a relationship between the meaning

of the home altar and the biblical tradition of effective divine presence
through immanence can bring the practitioner of the home altar devotion
into the world of biblical symbol and imagery. This would indeed be a
formidable challenge for the pastoral agent. However, some cautionary
notes are in order. One must not presuppose too much in evangelizing the
practitioners of religiosidad popular. Many have rural roots in an agricultural society and lack the needed prerequisites to comprehend the nuances
of modern biblical and hermeneutical methodology. The pastoral agent
must do plenty of preparatory work and then exercise judicious caution in
communicating the conclusions of the study. Also, the pastoral agent would
do well to take into account whatever cultural categories among Hispanics
could serve as vehicles for communication. For example, narrative or history
is more effective as a pedagogical tool with Hispanics than abstract concepts
in lecture-type formats.

ADVOCACY

The need for advocacy is great, to the extent that misunderstanding exists
in the official church regarding the home altar devotion. As with other
expressions of religiosidad popular, the home altar devotion can give the
impression of being aberrant and thus necessary to control. The pastoral
agent can be an effective advocate for this devotion by presenting to the
official church the merits and value of the devotion, and to the practitioners
the possibilities of deviation within the devotion unless there is ongoing
and fruitful dialogue with the official church. The pastoral agent best functions as a bridge between the official church and adherents of religiosidad
popular, presenting the values and possible excesses of the one to the other.

7

The Penitentes

EXPLANATION OF THE DEVOTION

The *Penitentes* are a brotherhood of laymen based primarily in northern New Mexico who have a special devotion to the sufferings and death of Jesus Christ that is focused primarily around Holy Week. The bulk of their private devotions takes place in a *morada*, which is usually an adobe building especially built for that purpose and is some distance from the parent church. There is a direct connection between the morada and the church building, since during Holy Week the Penitentes usually process from one to the other, showing some connection with the official church by participating in the official devotions of Holy Week, and also showing their apartness by having separate ritualization in the morada for the brotherhood only. Officially, they are known as *La Hermandad de Nuestro Padre Jesus Nazareno*, the Brotherhood of Our Father Jesus of Nazareth.

There are several theories as to their origins, but the most prominent seems to be that espoused by the historian Angelico Chavez. In one of his books on New Mexico, significantly titled *My Penitente Land*,[1] Chavez draws interesting topographic, historical, and religious parallels between biblical Palestine and New Mexico, thus setting up an image-laden analogical relationship between the Bible and New Mexico's religious history. Speaking of the origins of the Penitente devotion in New Mexico, Chavez describes Juan de Oñate's 1598 expedition into the Southwest and of the Holy Week celebration that year, which on Good Friday included, "... a well-established Spanish penitential feature of Lent—self-flagellation."[2] This penitential practice of self-flagellation was an accepted part of fervent Spanish piety. It was a practice not uncommon in Spain among male members of some religious orders and their lay affiliates called "Third Orders." It was a way of mortifying the flesh and doing penance for sin by imitating Christ's flagellation at the hands of Pilate before his death and crucifixion. Chavez summarizes it thus:

No one took it amiss—it was the Spanish soul at its most fervent. Back in Spain, in the period following the discovery of America, it was not uncommon for such pious societies or even the whole male congregation of a parish to go on public processions of blood even outside of Lent, as when plague or drought struck the countryside. The purpose was to placate what was considered to be God's anger, and as a result bring down his merciful blessings in the form of health or rain. The custom had come to the New World, and its excesses had later been proscribed on both sides of the ocean by combined royal and ecclesiastical decrees under heavy penalties.[3]

This Spanish devotion to the sufferings of Christ as a way of expiating for sin or placating the deity through specific penitential practice, including some form of flagellation, was very much a part of the religious message brought into the New World by the conquistadores. However, the more connected the devotional practices of the Penitentes became with the Bible, the more the idea shifted from placation of the deity to the gift of self through love that Jesus expressed by his death and resurrection. It was the motive of love, not placation of the deity, that gave Jesus' death and resurrection real significance. The cross was the fundamental Christian symbol that identified the follower of Jesus, so it was revered in as many ways as possible: as symbol dedicating a place to God, as standard in marches, as reminder of Jesus' redeeming suffering, death, and ultimate resurrection.

How did the Penitente brotherhood come into existence in northern New Mexico?[4] As is the case with any colonizing effort where the Catholic church is involved through her missionary enterprise, especially in Latin America, the clergy usually accompanied the conquistadores. So it was in 1598 when the Spaniard Juan de Oñate came through Mexico into what is now New Mexico, accompanied by Franciscan clergy who were to "evangelize" the natives. The stamp of Spanish piety together with a Franciscan spirituality was left on the Christianity that was taught, which included this profound devotion to the cross and sufferings of Christ. Over the years the lack of clergy allowed devotional piety to flourish in the natural amalgam of indigenous beliefs and Catholic doctrine as taught by the padres. The people's understanding of the Catholic doctrine was filtered through their cultural persona, which by the late eighteenth century was predominantly Hispanic settlers in remote villages, some of whom intermarried with Indians. Because of their remoteness and the lack of clergy, the people were, for the most part, left to their devices as far as their spirituality was concerned. As farmers and shepherds, the people were close to the earth and the rhythms of nature, and so were tuned in to sacred times, one of which was the springtime keyed into the lunar cycle. Holy Week and Easter were part of this sacred time of the lunar cycle. Thomas Steele and Rowena Rivera make the following observation:

For New Mexico, with its mainline medieval Franciscan spirituality, the Good Friday passion and death of Christ were especially the principal focus of sacred time . . . And so during these days the sacred focus of the village was in whatever place the people enacted for themselves a dramatic memorial of the passion and death, at first in and around the village chapel on the plaza, where they performed a passion play using large statues . . . to represent Christ, Mary, and John the Apostle. But we can only guess that these dramas were not dramatic enough to satisfy the people, and their dissatisfaction may have led them to begin forming at this time the Brotherhood of Our Father Jesus. And so toward the end of the eighteenth century or near the beginning of the nineteenth, the men of each village began to found chapters of *La Hermandad de Nuestro Padre Jesus Nazareno* and to make present the central events of the passion and death by themselves taking and suffering the part of Jesucristo. They embodied in their own bodies his agony, his scourging, his crowning with thorns, his carrying of the cross to Calvario, his being fastened to it and raised from the earth. Left to itself, the only operative religious body in the village did in this way what it could to make the village one with God.[5]

This nineteenth-century beginning of the Penitentes in northern New Mexico took root as basically a religious lay organization with subsequent political ramifications.[6] One of the earliest documented encounters between the official church and the brotherhood was during a pastoral visit in 1833 from Bishop Zubiría of Durango, Mexico, in whose ecclesiastical jurisdiction New Mexico subsisted. Bishop Zubiría became aware of what he felt were excessive abuses by the brotherhood and so issued a letter of warning to cease these abuses of excessive corporal penance and submit to ecclesiastical control. The brotherhood resisted because it was obvious to them that any kind of outside control meant lessening of autonomy over indigenous faith-expressions. So tensions between the brotherhood and the official church increased and continued.[7]

The Penitente devotion continues to this day in some of the villages of northern New Mexico, but certainly not to the extent that it flourished in the early part of this century. There are many reasons for this: growing urbanization, migration, consumerism, dilution of the Hispanic value system (especially with regard to family), and so on. Undoubtedly, one of the greatest reasons for the accelerating demise of this devotion, as with other devotions of religiosidad popular, is the lack of understanding of the cultural basis for the devotion, coupled with the failure of the practitioners of devotional piety and outsiders to dialogue intelligently, whether the outsiders were the official church representatives or the morbidly curious Anglos who sensationalized what they saw. Dialogue and understanding could enable a mutual enrichment to occur, as was the case with me when I spent Holy Week 1978 with a group of Penitentes in Arroyo Seco, New Mexico.[8]

The most memorable part of that experience was their apparent equanimity in the face of personal and community instances of adversity, and how their membership in the brotherhood was of such solace to them. I recall being impressed by their interpretive insights into those biblical passages that spoke directly to them. Consequently, in discussing the biblical analogues that follow, I want to make it clear that these analogues are the result of my own reflection, not that of the brotherhood.

BIBLICAL ANALOGUES TO THE PENITENTES

Historical and sociopolitical assessment of the Penitentes as a group sees them as representatives of a community coping with adversity. For Hispanic inhabitants of northern New Mexico from the late eighteenth century onward, there was much cause for experiencing adversity—from the harsh winters and frequently unyielding land to the expropriation of property by entrepreneurial Anglos. The experience of adversity was not uncommon in the Hispanic community of northern New Mexico.

Much as the early church confronted adversity through the literary genre of apocalyptic in order to give it hope and solace, so Hispanics in the southwestern United States have traditionally confronted adversity through religiosidad popular. Proposing the Penitentes as an example of Hispanic devotional piety with biblical analogues, albeit in the geographically constricted area of northern New Mexico, brings us biblically into the wisdom literature of TANAK, where we encounter two distinct perspectives on the experience of adversity. First there is the basic question of Job, "Why do the innocent suffer?" Then there is the apparent *carpe diem* attitude of Qoheleth, who says, "All things are vanity! Enjoy life such as it is." Both Job and Qoheleth challenged prevailing beliefs regarding reasons for suffering and experiencing adversity. The one view resigned itself to the inevitability of God's will; the other promoted the enjoyment of life within limits. We shall now examine both of these biblical perspectives as they deal with the issue of adversity.

THE PROBLEM OF JOB

The Book of Job belongs to a biblical genre known as wisdom literature, which differs markedly from works dealing with "salvation history" in that the wisdom literature concerns itself more with lived experience than with salvific events in history.[9] Job is generally considered to be at the very least an exilic work dealing with the universal question of why the innocent suffer. Israel's own experience of loss of Temple and monarchy, coupled with exile to a foreign land—the apparent failure of divine promises–left her in a state of psychological shock and theological trauma. How could Yahweh have abandoned his people after his promise to David that the Temple and monarchy would perdure *'ad 'ôlām* (forever) (2 Sam. 7)? There was no mistaking the effect it had on the people. The state of exile, away from Yahweh's protective presence, was truly an experience of adversity. It was in this context that Job was written as an attempt to deal with the very practical problem of the rationale behind the suffering of perceived innocence.

The phenomenon of the righteous sufferer was relatively widespread in the ancient Near East, particularly in Egypt and Mesopotamia. The Babylonian Theodicy and the Babylonian poem *Ludlul Bel Nemeqi* ("I will Praise the Lord of Wisdom"), as well as the Egyptian Dispute Over Suicide and the Satirical Letter of Hori are such examples.[10] At its root, the central issue at the time of Job was retribution. The prevailing belief was that the good prospered and the evil suffered. Evaluation was made from effect to cause; if an individual was prosperous, it was because he was blessed in God's eyes. That person had performed good deeds. Similarly, if a person suffered loss of property, health, or any other privation, it was because he was being punished by God. That person had committed some evil. However, the Book of Job was written to challenge the prevailing assumption that the good prospered and the evil were punished. The sages responsible for the Book of Job knew from personal experience that innocent people suffered, including children, for whom the punishment did not fit the crime. In the time of Jeremiah and Ezekiel, scarcely a century or two before the time of Job, there was already the firm belief in personal responsibility— each person was responsible for personal actions (Jer. 31:29–30; Ezek. 18:1–9, 30). Then why do the innocent suffer if they are guilty of no serious crime?

Several attempts at answering the question are presented by the friends of Job. The basic structure of the Book of Job is a series of disputations. There are three cycles of speeches between Job and his three friends, Eliphaz, Bildad, and Sophar (chapters 3–24), with interpolations by a brash young outsider named Elihu (chapters 32–37), and dialogue between Yahweh and Job (chapters 38–42). These cycles of speeches are written in poetry and are bounded by a prologue (chapters 1–2) and epilogue (chapter 42:7–17), both in prose. The prologue sets the scene for the disputations and the epilogue depicts the consequences. The argument proper is in the poetry text, the speeches.

One of the key difficulties of Job is the sense of Yahweh's justice. On the one hand, justice meant a salvific act that signified liberation from oppression for those in covenant relationship with Yahweh. On the other hand, if the covenant relationship were severed by the people, they experienced punishment and destruction. Covenant loyalty became a distinguishing characteristic of experiencing salvific justice. The crux of the problem lay in making precise the origin of justice. Was a just person such because of the quality of life he or she led, or was a person just because Yahweh declared him or her to be so? For Job this was a challenging question and a serious problem.

As becomes clear in the series of disputations, the problem of the innocent sufferer is tied in with the prevailing concept of retribution—reward
and punishment for corresponding behavior. Job's protagonists, operating
on the principle of retribution, deduce from effect to cause, thus provoking
Job's aggravated response protesting his innocence, which was a head-on
challenge to the retribution principle. For example, Eliphaz affirms that no
innocent person perishes (4:7), so if Job is punished, he must have committed sin, for sin brings about punishment (4:8–9). God finds faults in
everyone (4:17–19; 15:14–16), including Job (22:6–10). The purpose of
suffering is to correct (5:17–18) and eventually bring about prosperity
(5:19–26).

Bildad is much more direct in his argument. He agrees basically with
Eliphaz in affirming the tradition (8:8–10; 18:2–21) but also allows Job the
chance to "repent" for his sins—real or supposed (8:5–7). Sophar is quite
aggressive in his dealing with Job (11:3–6), especially as he reaffirms the
retribution principle from effect to cause (20:2–29). He does hold out hope
for Job by offering him a chance to "repent" (11:13–20), as did Bildad, in
case there are any sins that Job may have committed unwittingly.

Job more strongly and quite poignantly protests his innocence in the face
of these severe traditionalists (16:16–17; 30:24–31), and concludes that
there is a certain arbitrariness on God's part (13:15, 18, 23–28; 19:6–22).
Job experiences God as an enemy, or at the very least, a friend who has
abandoned him. In any case Yahweh is a silent God who remains hidden.[11]
Yet, in the midst of his suffering, Job believes that he has a *gô'ēl*, a vindi-
cator, who will fight successfully for his cause before God (19:25–27),
though it is not clear whether in this life or after death. Job has a firm
belief that true justice must somehow triumph in the end and so demands
to "have it out" with God. In their dialogue, God does not answer Job's
questions, but by affirming his own omnipotence makes Job aware of
dependency on him. Ultimately, God's response to Job is: "Who are you
to question my motives? I am not bound by your rules." This is a humbling
experience for Job, one that does not answer his deepest questions about
the reasons for his suffering, but does provide him with perspective in his
relationship with God. Marvin Pope, in his Job commentary, states:

> The complete evasion of the issue as Job had posed it must be the
> poet's oblique way of admitting that there is no satisfactory answer
> available to man, apart from faith. God does not need the help or
> advice of impotent or ignorant men to control the world, any more
> than he needed such to create it ... No extreme of suffering gives
> mere man license to question God's wisdom or justice as Job has
> done.[12]

God has not answered Job's question, nor has he blamed Job personally
for his adversity. In retrospect, the retribution argument of the three friends

seems to be rendered invalid, though not without some grudging recognition of its existence. After all, in the epilogue Job is restored his health and wealth far beyond his original condition, because when all was said and done, Job was innocent as he claimed.

What then are we left with in terms of an answer to the original question of why the innocent suffer? We have seen the broader ancient Near East experience of the innocent sufferer in the literature of Egypt and Babylonia, where the gods were considered responsible. Current thought at the time of Job offered various solutions: suffering as disciplinary, as a test, as punishment for a sin known or unknown, or as part of the universal human experience in a chaotic world. Job hints at another partial solution shared by Deutero-Isaiah in the songs of the Suffering Servant: individual innocent suffering is connected with the healing of the wider community. Marvin Pope states that 42:10 ". . . puts Job's restoration in a temporal and perhaps causal nexus with his intercessory prayer for his friends,"[13] thus linking Job's suffering with that of the Suffering Servant (Is. 53:10–12) as undergone for the benefit of others. It is unshakable faith in God's Providence and in his unfathomable will, especially in times of adversity, that the adversity itself can make any sense. Marvin Pope concludes, "Only by faith can such seeming defeat be turned to victory and the anguished cry, 'My God, why have you forsaken me?' give way to resignation and trust, 'Father into your hands I commend my spirit.' "[14]

THE CHALLENGE OF QOHELETH

On quite a different front, the biblical Book of Qoheleth, also called Ecclesiastes in its Greek form, presents a perspective unique in Hebrew wisdom literature.[15] The book comes from approximately the mid-third century B.C.E., a time when Israel's sages were aware of the effect of history and outside thought on Israel's own theology. On occasion, life experience contradicted established doctrine. In the case of Job, the established principle of retribution, especially as deduced from effect to cause, was directly and severely challenged because of the contrary life experience of the just man, Job. In the case of Qoheleth, the challenge to the accepted retribution principle was challenged on the more radical grounds that everything anyone did was futile. The kind of pessimism that seems to pervade Qoheleth appears to reject any kind of reward for good works. For Qoheleth, death cancels everything, therefore life has no meaning.

The central theme of the book appears in the very first verses: Everything is utter futility. The Hebrew word *hebel*, usually translated as "vanity," means a breath or vapor, something that is ephemeral and cannot be grasped because it is so temporary. Qoheleth, as an instructor on life's experiences, wanted to be certain that his listeners were aware of reality checks in life and were harboring no pious illusions. It was these reality checks that enabled Qoheleth to reflect on established ethical principles and challenge them if they did not correspond to his reality. We may say that Qoheleth represented the "liberal" wing of Israel's wisdom movement, while the Book of Proverbs, very neat in its categorizations of God's obligatory behavior, represented the "conservative" wing. Qoheleth was saying, as did Job, that God (Yahweh) cannot be compartmentalized in human categories and is free to reward or punish as he sees fit, not necessarily as we would like him to do. Qoheleth does not so much complain or deprecate as he critiques smug views on life. One of his major functions is to challenge existing ethical principles if they are at variance with lived reality.

The challenges of Qoheleth are basically four: death puts an end to everything; God is unknown; the world is fraudulent; and pleasure is recommended for its own sake.

That death puts an end to everything is apparent even to the casual observer of life. The wise man dies just as the fool dies (2:16), and all his ideas, plans, and possessions are taken up by others (2:18–19, 21). Both people and animals die, so there is no presumed human advantage, since both return to the dust whence they came (3:19–22). No one knows the day or hour of death (8:7–8; 9:12), for one fate befalls all (9:1–3), and the dead have nothing (9:5–6). By the same token, wisdom cannot reach its goal because everything is futile. Even the search for wisdom is vexatious (1:18).

Dealing with an unknown God is particularly painful for Qoheleth. It is not that God did not exist, but since his ways were unknowable so was he. God appears indifferent to human fate (3:18), therefore there is no room for a personal relationship. This is why there is no dialogue between Qoheleth and God, as there was between Job and God. Even though Job's relationship was contentious, at least it was a relationship that could be affected through dialogue. Perhaps Qoheleth had no relationship with God though he recognized God's power and the need for prudent behavior in the face of it (9:1ff.).

The world's fraudulence is practically a given if one bases one's life on established ethical principles. One's lived experience does not always fit neatly into these principles. For example, many of Qoheleth's predecessors in the Hebrew wisdom movement proposed the principle of retribution as almost a fixed law in the ethical universe. Suffering, poverty, and privation were consequences of divine disfavor or, more likely, punishment for sin. Wealth, health, and long life were consequences of divine favor or, more likely, reward for a virtuous life. However, both Job and Qoheleth challenged that. Qoheleth's challenge seems to be more radical than Job's in that while Job never lost his trust in God because of a personal relationship with him, the book's author eventually buys into the retribution principle by the ultimate divine restoration of Job's goods. Qoheleth cannot count on the fruits of a personal relationship, so he challenges the very foundations of the retribution principle. Qoheleth takes note of much oppression and pain in the world (3:16; 4:1–4) and knows experientially that though people themselves are responsible for some of it, other suffering has no direct attributable causality (7:15). Lest he come across as a confirmed pessimist, Qoheleth proposes a very positive alternative: the affirmation of life as fruits of God's blessings.

Almost as the single viable alternative to death as total annihilator, the unknowability of God, and the fraudulency of the world, Qoheleth proposes the pursuit of pleasure. This proposal is not so much a hedonistic magna carta as it is availing oneself of the singular benefits of God's creation. Since the future is unknowable and much in doubt, the present becomes the arena of challenge and affirmation. There is to be a sense of discipline in the pursuit of enjoyment, an awareness that pleasure also is futile (2:1–2), even though it is from the hand of God (2:24–25; 3:13–14). God means us to enjoy the fruits of his creation (5:18–20; 8:15) even though the joy is ephemeral. After all, enjoyment of life's pleasures is preferable to stagnation or death. It is also preferable to trust the validity of one's experience rather than the diaphanous theories of ideologues. Theories, especially ethical theories, must be constantly tested in the crucible of experience, and it is human experience that should shape the theory/principle, not the other way around.

In addition to affirming life, Qoheleth presents two other positive perspectives in the face of adversity. One is to accept the inevitable in life with some degree of equanimity; the other is to critique the false sense of religious security. The famous contemporary prayer "Serenity" could well have been penned by the hand of Qoheleth: "Lord, grant me the courage to change what I can, the serenity to accept the things I cannot, and the wisdom to know the difference." God's reasons for doing things are not for us to fathom. Like Job, Qoheleth maintains God's liberty and our ignorance of his motives. It is, after all, part of wisdom to accept life with courage and serenity and thus discover a hidden treasure, perhaps our own inner resources. The capacity to enjoy God's blessings in life, albeit in moderation, is a fundamental human value insofar as we recognize God as their source. Indeed, the fruit of wisdom lies not in solving the mysteries of life (and there are many) but in knowing how to live as well as possible under the difficulties and uncertainties of life. This is the challenge of Qoheleth, an ethic of faith that places our sense of trust in God's hands and accepts the results, rather than an ethic of rigid obedience that narrows our possibilities and God's choices.

In order to appreciate fully Qoheleth's value, it is necessary to distinguish between a "rejection" of God, which is what the atheist does, and a "challenge" of God's ways, which is what both Job and Qoheleth do. The challenge takes on various forms, one of which is critiquing accepted principles, particularly ethical principles, if they are at variance with lived experience. Uncritical attitudes lead to a sort of skewed understanding of a principle and thus to a false sense of religious security. The situation represented in Jeremiah 5:12 is a classic instance of a people's misunderstanding the original intent of a principle. The Israelite people in the early sixth century B.C.E. came to believe that Yahweh's unilateral covenant with David meant they were free of moral responsibility toward others and could exploit their neighbor. Jeremiah challenged this misunderstanding of the covenant, which led to a false sense of security. The acceptance of the inevitability of life with equanimity, the critiquing of a false sense of religious security, and the affirmation of life become Qoheleth's legacy to anyone who seeks a way to cope with adversities in life.

PENITENTES IN RELIGIOSIDAD POPULAR
REFLECTING ANALOGUES

We have seen in our biblical analogues that Job and Qoheleth have slightly different perspectives on coping with adversity. Job asks the question, "Why do the innocent suffer?" Though the question is not answered directly, Job's response is to accept the suffering with faith and trust in God, without impugning divine motives. Qoheleth, on the other hand, probes a little more deeply into the rationale for accepting the adversities in life. His response is first to question the legitimacy of the retribution principle by stating that the fate of all (good and bad) is the same. Death overcomes everyone, and thus all pursuits for fame, fortune, or whatever are futile. Consequently, attitude becomes important when bound to a view that affirms life as God intended it to be lived, by appreciating his blessings. The crucial attitude is one of seeing the present as the arena of one's control, and therefore of one's responsibility. Affirmation of life, through enjoyment of God's creation is the best way to deal with adversity, Qoheleth says. Since the benefits of creation are a given and are to be celebrated judiciously, they are the best one can hope for in a cruel world. A judicious celebration of life takes into account the acceptance of life's inevitabilities, which include adversity. After all, deprivation is merely the other side of blessing.

The Penitentes of northern New Mexico are not totally unlike the contemporaries of Job and Qoheleth. The harshness of life in the mountain villages of New Mexico, coupled with exploitative experiences from Anglo interlopers, gave them the feel for adversity. As with Job in his experience of adversity, the Penitentes, as is their custom, would accept their suffering as the will of God without probing into divine motivation. The devotion to the crucified Christ and Mary as *mater dolorosa* would provide acceptance of adversity with the requisite sense of equanimity. The brotherhood of the Penitentes did have, and most likely continues to have, a financial and emotional support system.[16]

Qoheleth's insights, though not yet evidenced to any extent among the Penitentes, could provide a very useful way to cope with the experience of adversity. First of all, the very notion of suffering, especially feelings of exploitation, could be questioned, particularly if the rationale for suffering is provided by outsiders to the community. Secondly, as with Qoheleth, so with the Penitentes there could be strong motivation to enjoy what God has given them—food, drink, family, friendships, and so forth (*disfrutar los bienes de la vida*). Since the sense of celebration is endemic to the Hispanic soul, the freedom to enjoy can be quite liberating. Because of this cultural postulate, it can be said that there is a paschal dimension to the Penitente devotions that is ultimately borne out through a theological study of the devotions themselves.[17]

With respect to the biblical hermeneutic of structuralism, we note the obvious existence of the affective dimension in the Penitente devotion. Certainly, any devotion professing and expressing the suffering Christ is derived from a most profound affective sense that enables the practitioner to identify more easily with the deep structure of the Job narrative as a whole. For example, the disruption of order for both Job and the Penitentes is the perceived injustice of the suffering or adversity. The attempt to reestablish order was for Job the various cycles of dialogue with his friends and with Yahweh. For the Penitentes, it is the attempt to come to grips with personal or communal adversity through means of the devotions during Holy Week. The reestablishment of order for Job was his dialogue with Yahweh and restoration of goods; for the Penitentes, it is whatever resolution they achieve as a result of reflection during devotions in Holy Week.

There is also some possible correlation with the deep structure of myth as the struggle between good and evil for both Job and the Penitentes. The chaos principle as a cause of evil in the world is an enigma, because no one is certain precisely who or what triggers its operation in the world. For Job, several reasons were given as the cause of his suffering, none of which he accepted as pertinent in his case. The chaos principle was overcome because of his trust in God and humble acceptance of God's will. For the Penitentes, the cultic experience of the devotions during Holy Week becomes the arena of struggle between the chaos principle, as the basic cause of adversity, and the victorious power of God as internalized in the ritualized belief of a positive outcome to Jesus' suffering and death. This is why a paschal dimension is so crucial to the Penitente devotion, so the devotee can express belief and relief that the chaos principle causing adversity has been overcome by the power of God, clearly present in the resurrection.

With respect to the biblical hermeneutic of reader-response criticism, we take into account both the attitudes and feelings that are communicated in the Penitente devotions as well as the semantic universe of the text that is applicable to the reader/hearer's context. The case of Qoheleth is applicable here. The critical attitude toward an accepted ethical principle at variance with experience, which was promoted by Qoheleth, could be very useful for the Penitentes in their coping with adversity. The skeptical challenge engenders reflection, which makes possible the ownership of consequences for one's actions or acceptance of the inevitabilities of life. Another attitude promoted by Qoheleth useful for the Penitentes is the enjoyment of life as partial solution to the challenge of coping with adversity. Life is to be enjoyed responsibly because it is a gift from God and a way of affirming his creation. Feelings of trust and confidence in God amid overwhelming odds are also engendered by this attitude promoted by Qoheleth.

The semantic universe surrounding the books of Job and Qoheleth is rich in symbolism that can readily be appropriated by the Penitentes. There is, for example, the symbolism in the prologue of Job with the fate of Job being discussed by God and the Adversary who will test Job. There is also the symbolism of character and content in the cycle of speeches between Job and his friends, each of whom provides an unacceptable reason for Job's suffering. There is, finally, the showdown between God and Job in a whirlwind. In the case of Qoheleth, the symbolism to be appropriated emerges out of the reader or hearer's understanding of the message of the text, for it is only in the interaction between the biblical text and the reader/hearer that there can be meaning for the Penitentes.

REVELATORY ASPECT OF THE PENITENTE RITUAL

As an expression of religiosidad popular, the Penitente ritual has its revelatory dimension. This ritual as devotion, concentrated primarily around Holy Week, embraces the traditions, history, and symbolization of the community experiencing the devotion. It is in this framework that revelation occurs.

The revelatory aspect of tradition resides in the interaction between memory and experience, which is interpretation. Adversity is a universal human experience, and memory of it continues to make present its significance for the moment when it is remembered. Memory as interpretative function can give a different meaning to each recollection of the experience of adversity. At one moment, the recollection can trigger frustration, anxiety, or anger, as it did for Job. Further recollection can trigger acceptance of the situation and compliance with the will of God. Yet further recollection can trigger critical response, subsequent dissatisfaction with conventional wisdom, and choice of an alternative, as was the case with Qoheleth. Each subsequent recollection of the adversity experience builds up the tradition, since the memory reinterprets the meaning for the given moment. And each remembrance can be considered revelatory. The Penitente ritual of Holy Week, with its primary focus on the sufferings of Christ, provides a suitable analogical relationship for reflection on learning to cope with adversity. For example, there may be in the community the memory of a fatal illness or tragic accident of some prominent person. Loss of income, property, or dispersion of family may have resulted from the loss. If the community has a Penitente brotherhood, there is likelihood that this experience of suffering and loss will be commemorated at some point in the Holy Week ritual. This consequence of suffering and loss, as a memory event, could be a revelatory experience for members of the community as the situation is personally applied.

The question of history as revelatory is answered in perceiving history as interpretative process rather than facticity. In the case of the Penitente devotions of Holy Week, different aspects of Christ's suffering that may not have fundament in facticity but do have meaning in their interpretation may be ritualized. This process is apparent, for example, in the currently accepted official devotion of the church of Christ's passion which is known as the Stations of the Cross. For example, the sixth station is the wiping of Jesus' face by Veronica while Jesus is carrying the cross to Calvary. There is no mention of Veronica in the canonical gospels, and there is no evidence that she was a historical personage. But her historical facticity is not the source of meaning for devotion to her. It is, rather, the significance of what she does: She overcomes her fear and overtly manifests compassion to a persecuted and suffering Christ at the risk of her own safety. Some spiritual writers frequently see this gesture as a model of behavior for us in the presence of injustice and oppression. If the official church can sanction such a meaningful gesture by a nonhistorical personage as part of her overall theology of the cross, surely the Penitentes in their Holy Week ritual can be allowed the same latitude in interpreting their understanding of the theology of the cross. The revelatory dimension of history in the Penitente ritual exists in the meaningful interpretation of something significant believed to have happened to the community or in the community as a result of divine activity and as commemorated during Holy Week. The difference between tradition and a sense of history with regard to revelation in the Penitente ritual is that the community tradition remembers a factual event, whereas the community sense of history commemorates a significant event that is only believed to have happened.

The revelatory dimension of symbolization is the involvement and transformation of the practitioner by means of the symbols of the devotion. With respect to the Penitentes there is much symbolization throughout the rituals of Holy Week, as in the processions from the church to the morada and back again symbolizing both connection with the official church and apartness. Then there is the rich symbolism of the ritual itself, frequently modified according to local tradition. The Arroyo Seco brotherhood, with whom I shared Holy Week, took the symbolism very seriously. On Wednesday of Holy Week, for example, the brothers spent the night in the morada, *vigilando a Jesus* — keeping watch with Jesus, commemorating the time in Gethsemane just before his arrest by Roman troops. Thursday and Friday were the focal days of Holy Week for the brotherhood, so they remained in the morada the whole time, handling their business, including induction of new members. The morada was the sacred space where special devotions were held, such as the Tenebrae ritual so common years ago during Holy Week in churches of the Latin rite. Every trip to the church for official liturgy, such as Mass, and back to the morada was a religious event — procession with candles and singing. Holy Thursday commemorated the last supper of Jesus with the apostles. During the Mass, members of the brotherhood served as the apostles. Good Friday was the occasion for other processions, chief of which was the way of the cross. Symbolism was rich and varied.[18] To the extent that the symbolization, wherever and however it was experienced during Holy Week, involved the Penitentes in the meaning of the sufferings of Christ and transformed them into better Christians, the symbolization was indeed revelatory.

We conclude by noting that the Penitentes' experiences of adversity, perceived as analogues to the illustrations from Job and Qoheleth mentioned above, serve as the framework for the faith-discourse, which is the dialogue with God to obtain meaning and understanding from the adversity. Whatever meaning is achieved from the faith-discourse becomes revelatory.

PASTORAL IMPLICATIONS

Pastoral implications with regard to the Penitentes tend to be somewhat limited because of localization of the devotion in northern New Mexico and southern Colorado and restricted access to the Penitentes themselves. Because of negative experiences with outsiders—people misunderstanding the nature of the devotion, resulting in bad publicity and a generally adversarial relationship with the institutional church—the Penitentes would not be a normal part of a typically Hispanic parish in the southwestern United States. Consequently, the pastoral suggestions that follow are directed primarily to those who have direct contact with them and secondarily to those who wish to understand them, or a similar geographically centered devotion, as persons of the church with a legitimate form of faith-expression. Acceptance remains the most basic and simple of the pastoral approaches. As chronicled by Weigle and Steele/Rivera,[19] the Penitentes have had a turbulent history in being understood and accepted. What has been said of the other practices of religiosidad popular is equally applicable to the Penitentes: Genuine understanding is based on accepting the validity of the cultural basis for the devotion as a genuine self-expression of belief in a special relationship with God. The folly of intolerance and lack of understanding proved to be costly pastoral mistakes.

Pedagogy and advocacy would be as applicable here as with the other devotional practices discussed earlier. Dialogue with the Penitentes involves listening to what their devotions have to say to those who inhabit a non-Hispanic world, and thus can be a teaching as well as a learning experience. Listening turns out to be one of the more effective pedagogical tools in any type of communication. Finally, advocacy would involve a prior understanding of the Penitente ritual and, where possible, pointing out to others its positive elements. Concretely, this would mean an attitude of openness about what the Penitentes have to offer our multicultural faith-experience as church, and promoting that understanding as part of the universal faith in God and his role in our history, a faith that is not limited by the rules and regulations of a single culturally bound institution, but as a faith allowed expression beyond those boundaries.

8

Conclusions

PROSPECTUS

The central argument of this book has been that there is a biblical basis for Hispanic devotional piety, also known as religiosidad popular, as it is practiced in the southwestern United States by Mexican Americans. This biblical basis provides a foundational legitimacy for religiosidad popular to be considered both as a rudiment for genuine spirituality and starting point for a Hispanic theology. Religiosidad popular, as a cultural phenomenon has as its constitutives traditions, a sense of history, and a symbolizing capacity. Its connection with the Bible is primarily through latent analogues that are brought to consciousness through the efforts of both the practitioners of religiosidad popular and the pastoral agents who minister to them.

The practitioners themselves recognize already established links with the Bible insofar as they are able to identify with and appropriate certain passages or personages. Pastoral agents help bring to conscious awareness dormant connections between religiosidad popular and the Bible through use of such tools as social sciences and hermeneutical methodology. Once this approach is utilized in order to obtain both a better understanding of the relationship between religiosidad popular and the official Catholic church and an appreciation of religiosidad popular's Hispanic roots, the next question is, where do we go from here? Is the value of religiosidad popular as a Hispanic expression of the Catholic faith limited by the boundaries of its Roman Catholicism and its cultural heritage? I would suggest that the value of religiosidad popular, in addition to affirming the cultural faith-expressions of Hispanics, goes beyond the boundaries of sectarianism and ethnicity. Two areas of exploration that take us beyond these boundaries to wider horizons are ecumenism and liberation.

RELIGIOSIDAD POPULAR AND ECUMENISM

It may seem strange to postulate an ecumenical value for religiosidad popular, given its strong Roman Catholic base. This value postulate is by no means a dilution of its significance within Roman Catholicism, but it is an assertion that religiosidad popular has value beyond its Roman Catholic moorings. One might object, then, that if this were the case it wouldn't make any difference to the Hispanic devotees of religiosidad popular which religion is professed as long as there was a belief in God expressed in a culturally affirming way. I would answer the objection by stating most emphatically that what I am suggesting as an ecumenical aperture for religiosidad popular is not a rejection of its Roman Catholic roots and connections, but an affirmation of those roots and connections by proposing two possibilities for enrichment.

One possibility is the broadening of the base for grounding religiosidad popular in Scripture if both Catholic and Protestant Hispanics who are devotees could engage in mutually illuminating dialogue. The other possibility is a similar broadening of the base for understanding dependent revelation. As we noted earlier in the treatment of revelation in chapter 3, foundational revelation is the basic deposit of faith of Catholic Christians. No one political, social, or religious group has a hammerlock on dependent revelation as a way of more clearly understanding foundational revelation.[1] Catholic and Protestant practitioners of religiosidad popular can learn from each other in terms of obtaining a deeper and more meaningful understanding of dependent revelation.

One of the more viable approaches to ecumenism and religiosidad popular as suggested here can be inferred from the recommended ecumenical approach proposed by the Methodist theologian Justo L. Gonzalez in his recent *Mañana: Christian Theology from a Hispanic Perspective*.[2] Gonzalez speaks of "reading the Bible in Spanish." By this he means reading the Bible not so much in Spanish translation as reading it from a Hispanic perspective. The Scriptures have a vital link to religiosidad popular, whether practiced by Catholics or Protestants. Gonzalez affirms a connection. "The great appeal of Protestantism was in Scripture itself, which the Catholic church had taught us to respect but not to read."[3] In fact, it was Protestants and Catholics mutually misunderstanding the relation of each other to the Bible that intensified their alienation and has led to suspicion.

There is, consequently, a need felt for a new kind of ecumenism, which Gonzalez expresses thus:

> The authority of Scripture is still held in high regard by that community [Protestant fundamentalists]. But there is also a growing awareness that there is a certain sort of fundamentalism that is grossly antibiblical. For this reason, many Protestants are seeking ways of interpreting Scripture that, while respecting the authority of the Bible, are different from what we were taught. The net result is that we find ourselves walking along the same path with Roman Catholics.[4]

The political and practical sides of this new ecumenism found expression in civil rights struggles and other social justice, common enterprises that helped remove the scales from the religiously biased eyes of both Catholics and Protestants.

The mediator of this new ecumenism is the Bible. The means of mediation is what Gonzalez calls "reading the Bible in Spanish," that is, reading the Bible from a Hispanic perspective. Part of that perspective views the Bible not as an idealized history of relationship between God and the people, but an actual history punctuated with sinfulness and retrogression after forgiveness. Similarly, the Hispanic experience in the United States is to be viewed not idealistically but realistically, as one of exploitation and suffering. It is the responsibility of Hispanics to remind the dominant group of its actual, not idealized, role in that history.[5]

Another part of the Hispanic perspective sees as a requirement for a truly Christian understanding of the Bible the need to value properly the significance of TANAK as principal resource for a valid understanding of the New Testament. There is an organic relationship between TANAK and the New Testament that must be recognized. We saw earlier how Hispanics were easily able to identify with TANAK because of its broad horizons of varied historical experience, life's vicissitudes, and human emotions, with which Hispanics could identify and subsequently appropriate. Gonzalez underscores the political nature of "reading the Bible in Spanish."

When the people read the Bible, and read from their own perspective rather than from the perspective of the powerful, the Bible becomes a mighty political book. This is what I mean by "reading the Bible in Spanish": a reading that includes the realization that the Bible is a political book; a reading in the "vernacular," not only in the cultural, linguistic sense but also in the socio-political sense.[6]

This new reading of the Bible necessitates a grammar appropriate to its purpose. Gonzalez offers the following four rules of grammar for the new reading.

"To say that the Bible is a political book means, first of all, that it deals with issues of power and powerlessness."[7] The issue of who has power and how it is used in relationship to God is one of the fundamental issues in Scripture. To read the Bible "in Spanish" means that Hispanics see themselves as powerless exiles outside the history of the dominant group.

"We must remember that only a small portion of Scripture was originally written to be read in private."[8] It is a mistake to think that the entire Scripture was written to or for individuals. This view leads to a privatization of the Bible's message. To read the Bible "in Spanish" means that whenever we read the Bible we must be aware that God is addressing us as a community of faith and we must shoulder responsibility to and for one another.

"We must remember that the core principle of scriptural 'grammar' is its availability to children, to the simple, to the poor."[9] Reading the Bible "in Spanish" has in view the understanding of Scripture provided by the simple, the poor. This perception is what Puebla referred to as the people's "evangelical instinct" that enables the practitioners of religiosidad popular spontaneously to sense what the Gospel is saying (448).

"Above all, however, we must learn to read Scripture in the vocative. The purpose of our common study of Scripture is not so much to interpret it as to allow it to interpret us and our situation."[10] To read the Bible "in Spanish" is to read it with the intention of allowing ourselves to be understood in light of the Word of God and see what God demands of us. On this issue Gonzalez has a significant point to make.

> At a certain level, this is the fundamentalist error: to believe that the path is *in* Scripture, that to penetrate Scripture is to walk with God, that the Bible is its own end. But this is also the error of much of biblical scholarship, which never returns from the written text to the context in which we must live today. If at the time of the Reformation Scripture was the captive of dogma and ecclesiastical authority, today it is often made the captive of historical criticism, textual analysis, form criticism, or whatever the latest word in biblical scholarship may be.
>
> The problem with such practices is not in the scholarship ... The problem is rather that they often take the Bible away from its proper function, which is to lead the people of God in their historical pilgrimage, and never return to that function.
>
> Reading the Bible "in the vocative" means reading with the clear awareness that we are not before a dead text, for the text that we address addresses us in return. It is in this manner that the Bible is most often read in Hispanic communities.[11]

The type of biblical interpretation that Gonzalez is calling for is the very sort suggested in this book for religiosidad popular: structuralism and reader-response criticism that focus more on the reader or hearer than on the text. In fact, all of the above rules of grammar for reading the Bible "in Spanish" can be applied to the biblical hermeneutic of religiosidad popular, as suggested in foregoing chapters of this work. For example, there is presented a communitarian stance to religiosidad popular's interpretation of the Bible; there is validity in a "simple" interpretation of Scriptures as described above; and in religiosidad popular the biblical text interprets the reader. The question of power and powerlessness, while ecumenical, is more easily contextualized within the framework of liberation.

RELIGIOSIDAD POPULAR AND LIBERATION

Liberation is one of those multifaceted concepts that have tended more toward obfuscation than to clarity the more the word is used. My intended use of the concept "liberation" within the context of religiosidad popular is taken from Puebla.

> Though the popular religiosity has set its seal on Latin American culture, it has not been sufficiently expressed in the organization of our societies and states. It has left standing what John Paul II has once again called "sinful structures." The gap between rich and poor, the menacing situation faced by the weakest, the injustices and the humiliating disregard and subjection endured by them radically contradict the values of personal dignity and solidary brotherhood. Yet *the people of Latin America carry these values in their hearts as imperatives received from the Gospel. That is why the religiosity of the Latin American people often is turned into a cry for true liberation.* It is an exigency that is still unmet. Motivated by their religiosity, however, the people create or utilize space for the practice of brotherhood in the more intimate areas of their lives together: e.g., the neighborhood, the village, their labor unions, and their recreational activities. *Rather than giving way to despair, they confidently and shrewdly wait for the right opportunities to move forward toward the liberation they so ardently desire* (452, italics mine).

Puebla's description of liberation as a logical outcome of religiosidad popular is stated in the following three propositions:

1. Religiosidad popular needs to be seen in its political dimension, that is, as in potential relationship to the "sinful structures" of society.

2. The values that challenge these societally sinful structures are imbedded in the hearts of the people from their exposure to the Gospel.

3. Religiosidad popular is the vehicle of response to this challenge, and the effect of the challenge is liberation. It is quite clear that the liberative dimension of religiosidad popular as described by Puebla is biblically based and societally oriented.

A second perception of the liberative potential of religiosidad popular is provided by Paul VI in *Evangelii Nuntiandi*. Though the holy father does not use the word *liberation* as a logical outcome of the exercise of religiosidad popular, it can be duly inferred from the following citation:

> It [religiosidad popular] can *arouse* in men a capacity for self-dedication and for the exercise in heroism when there is a question of professing the faith . . . It can *develop* inmost depths of man habits of virtue rarely to be found otherwise in the same degree, such as patience, acceptance of the Cross in daily life, detachment, openness to other men and a spirit of ready service (48, italics mine).

Though here presented as passive virtues, the capacities for arousal and development in religiosidad popular do indeed ultimately find flower in the self-affirmation that is true liberation.

Thus from Puebla and Paul VI we see the liberative potential of religiosidad popular as possibly confronting the sinful structures of society, being biblically based, and with a capacity to arouse and develop that potential. Our question now is, how does that liberative potential find effective expression? Before I attempt to answer the question, it is necessary to place in perspective the liberative potential of religiosidad popular.

Whenever we speak of liberation in relationship to any process, especially one of Hispanic origins such as religiosidad popular, we must see it within the framework of Latin American liberation theology as its methodological paradigm. Michael R. Candelaria, in a recently published monograph, *Popular Religion and Liberation: The Dilemma of Liberation Theology,*[12] posits a distinctive relationship between religiosidad popular and Latin American liberation theology when he says:

> In its attempt to articulate the contribution of faith to the struggle for liberation, the Theology of Liberation could not but turn to popular religiosity as a reservoir of the values and religious symbols of the people. Popular religiosity and the Theology of Liberation converge in their "capacity to humanize and to liberate social and cultural conditions."[13]

It is in positing the relationship that Candelaria brings to our attention the very division among some Latin American liberation theologians as to the value and significance of religiosidad popular. One position is represented by the Argentinian Juan Carlos Scannone,[14] and its opposite is defended by the Uruguayan Juan Luis Segundo.[15] "Scannone considers popular religion to be a contributing factor to liberation. Segundo berates popular religion as alienating, moribund, and incapable of being disestablishing."[16]

One of the major difficulties with Juan Luis Segundo's position regarding religiosidad popular is his virtual absolutism of the mass/minority dialectic, wherein he considers the "masses" as the multitudes of people characterized by uniformity and passivity, and the minority as the elites who are able to react effectively to history's realities and challenges.[17] Religiosidad popular, in Segundo's thinking, is generally the religious expression of the "masses," and a militant Christianity, which makes a difference in terms of change in a sinful world, is the religious expression of the "minority."

On the other hand, Juan Carlos Scannone has a much more positive view of religiosidad popular and its liberative potential, one very much in tune with Puebla (452). As background for his position on religiosidad popular, he recalls the 1969 San Miguel statement of the Argentinian episcopate, which stated that in the spirit of Medellín the church must involve and incarnate itself in the lives of the people, especially the poor people. Consequently, the activity of the church must be derived from the people, especially its liberative activity.[18]

Scannone believes that religiosidad popular, the "religiosity of the people" as he calls it, has liberative potential. One crucial criterion for determining this liberative potential is the experiential poverty and oppression of a people in a given historical situation. These poor people are normally practitioners of religiosidad popular who, in the experience of injustice and oppression, define oppressor, oppressed, and the situation of injustice.[19] Religiosidad popular, as a form of popular culture, is a way of living one's freedom insofar as it confronts its situation of oppression. Liberation methodology calls for a rereading of the Scriptures in light of the historical situation of oppression. Religiosidad popular's suggested biblical hermeneutic of structuralism and reader-response criticism allows practitioners of religiosidad popular to "re-read" or interpret anew for their own situation the biblical analogues and thereby encounter new meaning. The liberative dimension becomes incarnated through the new understanding taking place via the reinterpretation. I agree with Candelaria's summary of Scannone's position: "In its religious dimension, popular culture contains an openness to transcendence united with a sense of justice which can make a contribution to the praxis of liberation."[20]

Now I can answer the earlier question, how does the liberative potential of religiosidad popular find effective expression? Given the above discussion, I would respond by saying that it is principally the pastoral agent who can bring into relief the liberative potential of religiosidad popular and enable it to find effective expression. The pastoral agent is the person who, in his or her capacity as official representative of the church, has a direct pastoral relationship with the practitioners of religiosidad popular.

PASTORAL ORIENTATION

Over the years, pastoral efforts by the church with regard to Hispanics often have met with less than resounding success, particularly when dealing with religiosidad popular. As we saw in chapter 1, the relationship between the church and the Hispanic has generally been characterized by ambivalence and ambiguity. There always exists the opportunity for the church to ameliorate that relationship, especially through its representatives, the pastoral agents. I would like to offer some opportunities for pastoral agents in the form of specific suggestions. In chapters 4 through 7, the pastoral implications at the end of each chapter were specific suggestions rooted in the characteristics of the individual devotions. Here I would propose a plan. Above all, it is important to bear in mind that in a properly pastoral approach to religiosidad popular the pastoral agent, as official representative of the church, does not *give* the Hispanic anything, but rather brings to consciousness the promises for growth and development that are already present in the person and in the devotions. In fact, it may be said that the fundamental function, the pastoral priority of the pastoral agent, is to "unfold the potential" that is present in religiosidad popular. This unfolding (*desarrollar*) can take the following steps.

The first is to get to know the people in the sense suggested by *Ad Gentes*. The council document asks that when the church evangelizes through its missionaries, it

> *must be present* to these groups through those of its members who live among them or have been sent to them . . . In order to bear witness to Christ, fruitfully, they *should establish relationships of respect and love* with those men, they should *acknowledge themselves as members of the group* in which they live, and through the various undertakings and affairs of human life they should share in their social and cultural life. They *should be familiar with their national and religious traditions* and *uncover* with gladness and respect those *seeds of the Word* which lie *hidden* among them . . . Just as Christ penetrated to the hearts of men and by a truly human dialogue led them to the divine light, so too the disciples . . . should know and converse with those among whom they live . . . They must at the same time endeavor to *illuminate these riches with the light of the Gospel, set them free* and bring them once more under the dominion of God the savior (11, italics mine).

This form of knowledge and evangelization is, above all, a direct and committed accompaniment of the missioner (pastoral agent) with the people. Thus the first stage of development is called *accompaniment*, much the same way that Jesus accompanied people in their good times and bad. The force of the document's idea of accompaniment is to be present to the people in life's journeys of joy and sorrow. This form of accompaniment, as *Ad Gentes* shows, unfolds the riches of a people's culture, especially their religion, through the instrumentality of the Gospel, which gives it a liberative aspect as well.

The second stage for unfolding the potential of religiosidad popular by the pastoral agent is to remind the Hispanics of their history and help them come to grips with it. This stage is called *re-memorization*. One's view of reality and self is conditioned by whether one sees the self as subject or object of that history. Am I an actor, or am I being acted upon? Do I define myself and my role in history, or do others do it for me? The answer to these and similar questions will determine whether I am an object or subject in my own history. If an object, then a transformation is needed in order to become a subject. The pastoral agent can help the Hispanic with this transformation by helping to bring to consciousness the joys and sorrows of the past, including the experiences of oppression, that are sometimes commemorated in certain devotions of religiosidad popular, and then ask the why of these experiences. Through this re-memorization process, people tend to understand more clearly their traditions, and therefore themselves. Perhaps the most useful part of this stage of unfolding the potential is for the pastoral agent to impress on the people the importance of asking "why" as they remember their traditions, especially those that evoke pain and sorrow.

The third stage in unfolding the potential is what I would call the stage of *biblical resource*. This means, first of all, that the pastoral agent and the practitioners of religiosidad popular affirm the already existing relationship between the Bible and religiosidad popular. Secondly, the pastoral agent enables the people to discover biblical analogues in whatever devotion is under consideration through the use of pertinent biblical methodology and appropriate social sciences. The biblical analogues provide a framework for the discovery of revelatory potential in the devotions. Thirdly, the pastoral agent helps unfold the liberative potential of religiosidad popular and thus gives expression to its social dimension. The liberative potential can unfold through employment of Gonzalez's grammatical rules for "reading the Bible in Spanish," and, more importantly, through employment of Puebla's three propositions for liberation on the part of religiosidad popular, the second of which provides the biblical basis, namely:

1. Religiosidad popular needs to be seen in its political dimension, that is, as in potential relationship to the "sinful structures" of society.

2. The values that challenge these societally sinful structures are imbedded in the heart of the people from their exposure to the Gospel.

3. Religiosidad popular is the vehicle of response to this challenge, which effect is liberation.

The pastoral suggestions in this chapter are offered as a plan or a pattern of approach that can deal with a number of devotions. But regardless of specific plans or particular recommendations for better understanding and appreciating religiosidad popular, my ultimate hope is that those who read it and work with Hispanics and assist them to go beyond the boundaries of their devotions will themselves also be motivated to go beyond the boundaries of whatever inhibits them, so that they can be more effective pastoral agents.

Notes

INTRODUCTION

1. For a more detailed view of theological reflections on devotional practices in the Southwest, see Rev. Juan Romero, ed., *Faith Expressions of Hispanics in the Southwest*, vol. 1, in workshops on Hispanic Liturgy and Popular Piety (San Antonio, Tex.: Mexican American Cultural Center, 1979).

2. This workshop in Albuquerque was the second of three workshops on the theme of religiosidad popular. The first was held in San Antonio, Texas; the third in Los Angeles, California. All three workshops featured Luis Maldonado, a Spanish theologian who is a recognized expert in religiosidad popular. The workshops were organized by Rev. Juan Romero, and the results were published in his monograph cited in note 1, above.

3. Our method was to meet separately with our "target groups" that crossed the spectrum of age, economic status, education, rural/urban areas, in the general New Mexico region, and have them focus on a single devotional practice that was meaningful to all in the group. Then we, the pastoral agents, met monthly to reflect on these devotional practices within the context of common threads from the perspectives of pastoral experience, anthropology, theology, and scriptural themes. The results gave us a better understanding of the people's worship and belief practices, and was most useful for subsequent evangelization.

4. Segundo Galilea, *Religiosidad Popular y Pastoral Hispano-Americana* (New York: Centro Católico de Pastoral Para Hispanos del Nordeste, Inc., 1981).

5. An insightful and useful overall review of eight recent books written by Hispanics on a wide spectrum of issues in Hispanic theology is provided by Fernando Segovia, "A New Manifest Destiny: The Emerging Theological Voice of Hispanic Americans," *Religious Studies Review*, April 1991. A helpful work discussing customs and themes in Spain that show remarkable parallels to devotional practices among Hispanics in the southwestern United States is by William A. Christian, Jr., *Local Religion in Sixteenth-Century Spain* (Princeton, N.J.: Princeton University Press, 1981). See especially his treatment of vows, shrines, and local (urban) devotions.

6. Moises Sandoval, *On the Move: A History of the Hispanic Church in the United States* (Maryknoll, N.Y.: Orbis Books, 1990).

1. THE CHURCH AND THE HISPANIC

1. Enrique Dussel documents this so clearly in his classic work *Historia de la Iglesia en America Latina, Coloniaje y Liberación, 1492–1973* (Barcelona: Nova Terra, 1974). English translation is: *A History of the Church in Latin America: Colo-*

nialism to Liberation, 1492–1979 (Grand Rapids, Mich.: Eerdmans, 1981). Citations will be taken from the English translation.

2. Dussel, pp. 75–123.

3. Dussel, p. 69.

4. Dussel discusses the crisis within what he calls "popular Catholicism" that sheds light on the fate of Latin American devotional piety in its politicized dimension. Dussel, pp. 82–86.

5. This term "nonconformist" can refer to a spectrum of differences, whether they be language, customs, traditions, or, more importantly, differences in forms of devotion. Orthodoxy and orthopraxis, i.e. that which was considered "conformist" in belief and behavior, were generally defined by the dominant Anglo-Irish hierarchy.

6. This could be documented in every diocese in the country where a sizable Hispanic Catholic population exists. See, for example, Antonio Stevens Arroyo, *Prophets Denied Honor* (Maryknoll, New York: Orbis Books, 1981), and Sandoval, *On the Move*.

7. This was the first of the documents promoted by the Second Vatican Council (1962–1965) that indicated the importance given to liturgy and the need for liturgical reform.

8. Luis Maldonado, *Introducción a la Religiosidad Popular* (Santander: Sal Terrae, 1985), p. 197.

9. Maldonado, pp. 195–96.

10. Maldonado, p. 194. For an extensive discussion of the historical relationship between the church and devotional piety in the Americas, see Maldonado, pp. 35–58.

11. Letter from Avery Dulles to author, July 2, 1990.

12. Austin Flannery, ed., *Vatican Council II: The Conciliar and Postconciliar Documents* (Collegeville: Liturgical Press, 1984), p. 13. Citations of conciliar documents taken from this volume will be referred to as Flannery, vol. 1.

13. Austin Flannery, ed., *Vatican Council II: More Postconciliar Documents*, vol. 2 (Northport, New York: Costello, 1982), pp. 711–61. Citations from this volume will be referred to as Flannery, vol. 2.

14. Flannery, vol. 2, p. 732.

15. Flannery, vol. 1, pp. 903–1014. Citations from the document are given according to paragraph numbers.

16. "Conclusiones," *La Iglesia en la Actual Transformación de America Latina a la Luz del Concilio*, vol. 2 (Bogota: CELAM, 1970). Another version of the conclusions from Medellín may be found in *Medellín: Conclusiones. Segunda Conferencia General del Episcopado Latinoamericano* (Lima: Ediciones Paulinas, 1986). The document on *Pastoral Popular* is rather short, only fifteen paragraphs divided into three parts: *Situación, Principios Teológicos,* and *Recomendaciones Pastorales*.

17. Paragraph citations are taken from the final Puebla document as found in *Puebla and Beyond*, eds. J. Eagleson and P. Scharper (Maryknoll, New York: Orbis Books, 1979).

18. This semantic issue will be developed at greater length in the next chapter.

19. This emphasis on knowledge of the symbols in devotional piety seems to me to be the key for a theological validation of devotional piety.

20. As the United States bishops recognized in their pastoral letter on Hispanic ministry, *The Hispanic Presence: Challenge and Commitment* (Washington, D.C.: U.S.

Catholic Conference, 1984), p. 25. They say, "Hispanics in our midst are as yet an untapped resource as a cultural bridge between North and South in the Americas. The wellspring of Hispanic culture and faith is historically and geographically located in Latin America. For this reason, a dynamic response to the Hispanic presence in the United States will necessarily entail an even greater understanding and linkage with Latin American society and church."

21. National Conference of Catholic Bishops, *National Pastoral Plan for Hispanic Ministry* (Washington, D.C.: U.S. Catholic Conference, 1987).

22. The *Tercer Encuentro* took place on August 15–18, 1985, in Washington, D.C., organized principally by Rev. Juan Romero. It was the culmination of a long process of national consultation on many levels from and by Hispanics in every echelon of the church in the United States. The *Tercer Encuentro* well represents the hopes and aspirations of United States Hispanics with regard to the Catholic church. Summaries of the process and conclusions can be found in *Prophetic Voices* (Washington, D.C.: The Secretariat for Hispanic Affairs, U.S. Catholic Conference, 1986).

23. Pastoral letter on Hispanic ministry (Washington, D.C.: National Conference of Catholic Bishops, 1983).

24. *National Pastoral Plan for Hispanic Ministry*, pp. 4–5.

25. *The Hispanic Presence*, pp. 25–26.

26. *The Hispanic Presence*, pp. 26–27.

2. THE BIBLE AND DEVOTIONAL PIETY

1. In my home diocese of Los Angeles, California, the percentage of Spanish speaking is approaching something like 60% out of some 3.5 million Catholics. Among these Hispanic Catholics there are many refugees from Central and South America. Currently, the majority of Catholic Hispanics in the Los Angeles area is from Mexico.

2. Though Mexicans are often considered Latin Americans, their geographical proximity to the southwestern United States gives them a special status that enables them to exercise a particular influence on the religious and cultural life of United States Hispanic Catholicism. Hence I posit a distinction in theological impact between Mexico and Latin America with regard to southwestern Hispanic devotional piety.

3. There were others, e.g. the national episcopate of Argentina in April 1969 and the CELAM synod of bishops in March 1974 to cite two.

4. Although some Latin American theologians writing on the subject preferred the term *Catolicismo popular*.

5. See Sandoval, *On the Move*, pp. 7–22, for numbers and geographical distribution within a historical and sociopolitical context.

6. Luis Medina Asencio, "El Derecho Indigena de Nueva España," *La Religiosidad Popular en Mexico*, ed. Mexican Theological Society (Mexico: Ediciones Paulinas, 1975), pp. 139–49. There are a number of useful articles in this collection regarding the history of religiosidad popular and faith in Mexico, e.g. as promoted by the Augustinians and the Franciscans.

7. Dussel, *A History of the Church*.

8. Raul Vidales, "Sacramentos y Religiosidad Popular," *Servir* 10:52 (1954), p. 358.

9. Which we will do in the next chapter.

10. Javier Lozano Barragán, "Religiosidad Popular y sentido de la fe del Pueblo de Dios," *La Religiosidad Popular en Mexico*, ed. Mexican Theological Society (Mexico City: Ediciones Paulinas, 1975), p. 178. This view attempts to bring a balance to the acknowledged heavy emotional context of devotional piety.

11. An excellent assessment of the ambiguities of devotional piety is done by Ernest Henan, "Popular Religiosity and Christian Faith," in *Popular Religion*, Concilium, no. 186, eds. Norbert Greinacher and Norbert Mette (Edinburgh: T & T Clark, 1986), pp. 76–80.

12. Henan, p. 80.

13. Segundo Galilea, "La fe como principio crítico de promoción de la religiosidad popular," *Mision Abierta* 8/9 (Sept./Oct. 1972), pp. 426–37. The following comments are based on Galilea's observations.

14. Galilea, pp. 426–37, offers some very concrete suggestions from a pastoral perspective on how to develop the faith critique with respect to religiosidad popular.

15. TANAK is an acronym for the Hebrew Scriptures: *Torah* (the Law), *Nebii'm* (the Prophets), and *Kethubim* (the writings). The term "Old Testament" is a Christian designation for TANAK. Modern Christian biblical scholarship is displaying greater sensitivity to Jewish colleagues by the use of this term as well as the sigla used for dating biblical events: B.C.E. (before the common era), which Christians were accustomed to see as B.C. (before Christ). Obviously this usage is merely a literary tool and does not make a faith statement.

16. Raul Vidales, "Sacramentos y Religiosidad Popular," *Servir* 4: 52 (1974), p. 368.

17. Herman Vorländer, "Aspects of Popular Religion in the Old Testament," *Popular Religion*, Concilium, no. 186, eds. N. Greinacher and N. Mette (Edinburgh: T & T Clark, 1986), pp. 63–70. Vorländer, despite some negative criticism of popular religion, has an overall positive view of it. "Popular religion emphasizes the aspect of nearness to human existence by closely linking the experience of God and the experiences of life. Faith in Yahweh becomes remote from life, theoretical, unless it is continually enriched by the influence of popular religion" (p. 70).

18. Foremost among modern exponents has been Norman Gottwald. See, for example, his classic work *The Tribes of Yahweh* (Maryknoll, New York: Orbis Books, 1979) and his sociological introduction to the Hebrew Bible entitled *The Hebrew Bible: A Socio-Literary Introduction* (Philadelphia: Fortress Press, 1985). Witness also the growth of sections in the Society of Biblical Literature at annual meetings on sociology and the Bible.

19. Charles H. Kraft, "Supracultural Meanings via Cultural Forms," *A Guide to Contemporary Hermeneutics*, ed. Donald K. McKim (Grand Rapids, Mich.: Eerdmans, 1986), p. 314. This article is reprinted from Kraft's larger opus, *Christianity in Culture: A Study in Dynamic Biblical Theologizing in Cross Cultural Perspective* (Maryknoll, N.Y.: Orbis Books, 1979), pp. 116–46.

20. As mentioned by Kraft, "Supracultural Meanings," p. 319.

21. Kraft, "Supracultural Meanings," pp. 320–21. Kraft here expands on the suggestions made by Eugene Nida.

22. Kraft, "Supracultural Meanings," p. 333.

23. Kraft, "Supracultural Meanings," pp. 335–43, where he discusses the issue thoroughly, complete with diagrams.

24. Bruce Malina, *The New Testament World: Insights from Cultural Anthropology*

(Atlanta, Ga.: John Knox Press, 1981). See also Clifford Geertz, *The Interpretation of Cultures* (New York: Basic Books, 1973).

25. Malina, p. 23.

26. Malina, p. 21.

27. Malina, p. 22.

28. A term proposed by the Englishman H. Wheeler Robinson to describe the situation where the community was represented by the individual in terms of both blessing and punishment, e.g. blessings to Abraham (Gen. 12) and curses to individuals (Joshua 8). Robinson's notion of corporate personality has been challenged by scholars, most recently by John W. Rogerson, "The Hebrew Conception of Corporate Personality: A Re-examination," *Anthropological Approaches to the Old Testament*, ed. Bernhard Lang (Philadelphia: Fortress Press, 1985), pp. 43–59.

29. Cultural anthropology calls this phenomenon "dyadism." The "dyadic personality" is explained more in detail in Malina, *New Testament World*, pp. 53–60.

30. Malina discusses the issue of limited good in chapter 4 of his work, and has an interesting discussion on the notion of causality that could also bear on Hispanic devotional piety. Malina, *New Testament World*, pp. 88–89. The concept of "limited good" was originated by George Foster, in his seminal article; "Peasant Society and the Image of Limited Good," *American Anthropologist* 67 (1965), pp. 293–315. Thanks to N. Wellmeier for this reference.

31. Malina, p. 117.

32. Ibid.

33. Malina, pp. 105–18.

34. First suggested by James Muilenburg in his presidential address to the Society of Biblical Literature in 1968. See "Form Criticism and Beyond," *Journal of Biblical Literature* 88 (1969), pp. 1–18.

35. An excellent work which discusses these new methods in detail is Terence J. Keegan, *Interpreting the Bible: A Popular Introduction to Biblical Hermeneutics* (New York: Paulist Press, 1985). In addition to structuralism and reader-response criticism, Keegan also discusses at length "canonical criticism." My problem with canonical criticism as a viable model is that the canonizing process requires an authority for canonization whose identity the canon-critics don't quite seem to make clear. In current Christianity, Protestants and Catholics have very distinct lines of authority within their religious traditions as to who "calls the shots." There is no doubt in the Catholic's mind where the authority for a book's canonization lies. Further discussion of structuralism and reader-response criticism will be based on Keegan's observations. A more comprehensive discussion of reader-response criticism may be found in Edgar V. McKnight, *Post-Modern Use of the Bible: The Emergence of Reader-Oriented Criticism* (Nashville, Tenn.: Abingdon Press, 1988). For a more extensive treatment on biblical structuralism, see Robert M. Polzin, *Biblical Structuralism. Method and Subjectivity in the Study of Ancient Texts* (Philadelphia: Fortress Press, 1977).

36. Keegan, *Interpreting the Bible*, pp. 41, 43.

37. Keegan, p. 45.

38. Keegan, p. 61.

39. This method is discussed at length in Keegan, *Interpreting the Bible*, pp. 73–90.

40. Keegan, pp. 75, 76.

41. Keegan, p. 77.

42. Keegan, p. 82.

43. Keegan develops the reader-response method by discussing narrative-criticism as the logical outcome of reader-response, with particular reference to narratives in the Bible. Keegan, chapter 6.

44. Vidales, "Sacramentos y Religiosidad Popular," p. 373.

45. Raul Duarte Castillo, "Utilización de Ciertas Formas Populares en la Religiosidad Biblica," *La Religiosidad Popular en Mexico*, ed. Mexican Theological Society (Mexico City: Ediciones Paulinas, 1975), pp. 165–72.

46. Barragán, "Religiosidad Popular," pp. 177–79.

47. The German scholar Martin Noth often applied this principle in his classic study on the Pentateuch.

3. REVELATION AND RELIGIOSIDAD POPULAR

1. Paul Tillich, *Systematic Theology*, vol. 1 (Chicago: University of Chicago Press, 1951), p. 127.

2. John Macquarrie, *Principles of Christian Theology* (New York: Chas. Scribner's Sons, 1966), p. 7.

3. Ibid.

4. Macquarrie, p. 12.

5. Macquarrie, p. 8.

6. Gerald O'Collins, *Fundamental Theology* (New York: Paulist Press, 1981), p. 101. I'm grateful to Avery Dulles for calling to my attention the positions of Tillich, Macquarrie, and O'Collins regarding revelation.

7. Avery Dulles, *Models of Revelation* (Garden City, N.Y.: Doubleday Image, 1985), p. ix.

8. The meaning of a word is culturally conditioned and could give insight into a people's understanding of their own reality as, for example, studies on the key words for "revelation" in the Bible; *glh* in Hebrew and *apokalupto* in Greek. See Hans Jürgen Zobel, "Galah," in *Theological Dictionary of the Old Testament*, eds. G.J. Botterweck and H. Ringgren, vol. 2 (Grand Rapids, Mich.: Eerdmans, 1975), pp. 476–88; Albrecht Oepke, "Apokalupto," in *Theological Dictionary of the New Testament*, ed. G. Kittel, vol. 3 (Grand Rapids, Mich.: Eerdmans, 1965), pp. 563–92.

9. This distinction is important in order to appreciate the contribution of both "process" and "content" in tradition. Also, an analysis of tradition as probable locus of revelation is necessary to broaden the scope of understanding beyond the biblical text itself. The evangelist John seemed to hint at this in Jn. 21:25. See also Gerard Owens, "Is All Revelation Contained in Scripture?" in Faculté de Theologie Université de Montreal, *Studia Montis Regii*, vol. 1 (1958), pp. 55–60.

10. Douglas A. Knight, "Revelation through Tradition," *Tradition and Theology in the Old Testament* (Philadelphia: Fortress Press, 1977), p. 144.

11. See, for example, the classic studies on the subject. Gerhard von Rad, "The Origin of the Concept of the Day of Yahweh," *Journal of Semitic Studies* 4 (1959), pp. 97–108; Sigmund Mowinckel, *He That Cometh* (Nashville, Tenn.: Abingdon Press, 1954), pp. 109–392; and the bibliography cited by A. J. Everson, "Day of the Lord," *Interpreter's Dictionary of the Bible: Supplement* (Nashville, Tenn.: Abingdon Press, 1976), pp. 209–10.

12. An important article on the subject was written by Martin Noth, "The Re-

Presentation of the Old Testament in Proclamation," *Essays on Old Testament Hermeneutics*, ed. Claus Westermann (Richmond: John Knox, 1966), pp. 76–88.

13. Knight, "Revelation Through Tradition," p. 167, footnote 41.

14. Knight, p. 179. This whole paragraph reflects Knight.

15. The Bible is the sole literary context where for us Christians the question of the relationship between history and divine revelation is theologically dealt with, and so becomes relevant and crucial to our discussion.

16. G. Ernest Wright, *God Who Acts: Biblical Theology as Recital* (Chicago: Alec Allenson, 1952). When it came out, this book was pivotal in the thinking of many Scripture scholars, especially those who espoused the "Biblical Theology" movement.

17. Wolfhart Pannenberg, *Revelation as History* (New York: Macmillan, 1968). Originally published as *Offenbarung als Geschichte* (Göttingen: Vandenhoeck und Ruprecht, 1961). In this work, edited by Pannenberg, scholars from different theological disciplines address the issue of revelation as history. See especially the article by Rolf Rendtorff, "The Concept of Revelation in Ancient Israel," pp. 23–53. Pannenberg's work precipitated scholarly discussion in the United States on the subject of the relationship between history and theology. See, for example, J.M. Robinson and J.B. Cobb, eds., *Theology as History*, (New York: Harper & Row, 1967); R. Funk, ed., *History and Hermeneutic* (New York: Harper & Row, 1967).

18. James Barr, "Revelation through History in the Old Testament and in Modern Theology," *Interpretation* 17 (1963), pp. 193–205. This was Barr's key essay, to be followed by such works as "The Concepts of History and Revelation," in *Old and New in Interpretation* (New York: Harper & Row, 1966), pp. 65–102.

19. Werner Lemke, "Revelation through History in Biblical Theology," *Interpretation* 36 (1982), pp. 34–46.

20. Lemke, p. 45.

21. Dulles, *Models of Revelation*, p. 132.

22. On the subject of nonliterary revelation, see the useful article by Rene Latourelle, "La Révélation comme Parole, Témoinage, et Recontre," *Gregorianum* 43 (1962), pp. 39–54. Dulles also speaks to the revelatory aspect of ritual in his quote of John Macquarrie. Dulles, *Models*, pp. 134, 140.

23. Dulles, p. 135.

24. Dulles, p. 280.

25. Dulles, p. 281.

26. See, for example, Paul Ricoeur, *Biblical Interpretation* (Philadelphia: Fortress, 1980), edited with L. Mudge; *Interpretation Theory: Discourse and the Surplus of Meaning* (Fort Worth: Texas Christian University, 1976); *The Bible as a Document of the University* (Chico, California: Scholars Press, 1980), in joint authorship with Gerhard Ebeling and James Barr, and edited by Hans Dieter Betz. In addition, the works of Severino Croatto, an important Argentinian biblical scholar who works on literary theory, show the heavy influence of Ricoeur.

27. The following argument is based on Paul Ricoeur, "Toward a Hermeneutic of the Idea of Revelation," *Harvard Theological Review* 70 (1977), pp. 1–37.

28. Ricoeur, p. 15.

29. Ricoeur, p. 16.

30. These would be the autonomy of the text, the externality of the "work" (the shaping of the faith-discourse), and the transcendent world of the text, all of which open up the world of understanding between text and reader.

31. Ricoeur, p. 23.

32. There is a certain psychology involved in understanding revelation that needs to be considered. This is provocatively dealt with in B. Gemser, "Delayed Consciousness of Revelation," *Adhuc Loquitur: The Collected Essays of B. Gemser*, A. Van Selms, ed., Pretoria Oriental Series, vol. 7 (Leiden: E. J. Brill, 1968), pp. 150–76.

33. Except those devotions connected to the Guadalupe in Spain, who, according to some scholars, is antecedent to and independent of Guadalupe in Mexico.

34. There are a significant number of this type of "apparition" among Hispanics in the Southwest, though most of them receive only limited local media coverage. The classic example of Our Lady of Guadalupe and the recipient of the apparition, Juan Diego, also raises the issue of facticity vs. belief to a new level. Despite the fact that Juan Diego was beatified by Pope John Paul in May 1990, some historians challenge his facticity as a historical personage. This challenge does not affect the results of the faith-factor concerning Juan Diego, however. Many still believe in him and pray for his intercession. See *Los Angeles Times*, May 12, 1990, F: 18.

35. Dulles, *Models*, pp. 136–39.

36. Dulles, pp. 136–37. He quotes Victor White, a Jungian disciple, on the beneficially therapeutic effect of healing through symbol.

37. An argument can be made for any language to be given special status, as long as it is directly connected with sacred ritual. Because of its sacrality in cult, language tends to become fixed in formulas and tends to resist any form of change.

38 J. Severino Croatto, *Biblical Hermeneutics: Towards a Theory of Reading as the Production of Meaning* (Maryknoll, New York: Orbis Books, 1987). Many pertinent works are cited therein.

39. The Argentinian theologian Juan Carlos Scannone speaks of popular culture, with specific reference to Latin America and liberation, as a hermeneutic locale. Juan Carlos Scannone, "Theology, Popular Culture, and Discernment," *Frontiers of Theology in Latin America*, ed. Rosino Gibellini (Maryknoll, New York: Orbis Books, 1979), pp. 213–39, esp. pp. 222–25.

4. ASH WEDNESDAY

1. For a critical study of Ezekiel 28 that deals with the theme of creation, see the commentary by Walther Zimmerli, *Ezekiel 2*, Hermeneia (Philadelphia: Fortress Press, 1983), pp. 72–101. Biblical citations henceforth will be taken from the *Revised Standard Version* published by Thos. Nelson and Sons, N.Y., 1952, unless otherwise noted.

2. As described by Walther Eichrodt, *Ezekiel* (Philadelphia: Westminster, 1970), pp. 390–95.

3. This last phrase is the formula often used at the ceremony of the distribution of ashes on Ash Wednesday.

4. Note that the serpent is also punished by having to eat dust (*'āfār*), (Gen. 3:14).

5. This linkage of true penitential practice with the doing of justice is part of the ancient prophetic tradition announced by Amos, Hosea, and Isaiah with regard to abuses in the cult. Cf. Amos 5:21–25; Hosea 8:11–13; Isaiah 1:11–17.

6. The rise and development of apocalyptic during biblical times is significant in the history and theology of Israel. See the helpful studies of D. S. Russell, *The*

Method and Message of Jewish Apocalyptic (Philadelphia: Westminster, 1964); H. H. Rowley, *The Relevance of Apocalyptic* (New York: Association, 1964); Paul Hanson, *The Dawn of Apocalyptic* (Philadelphia: Fortress Press, 1975); R. W. Funk, "Apocalypticism," *Journal for Theology and Church* (New York: Herder and Herder, 1969).

7. See illuminating commentary on this chapter in A. Lacoque, *The Book of Daniel* (Atlanta, Ga.: John Knox Press, 1979), pp. 177–99.

8. In place of ashes the Septuagint has Job sitting on a dunghill (*koprías*) outside the city.

9. See, for example, the Babylonian *Ludlul Bel Nemequi* ("I Will Praise the Lord of Wisdom"); "A Pessimistic Dialogue between Master and Servant"; "A Dialogue about Human Misery," in James B. Pritchard, *Ancient Near Eastern Texts*, 2d ed. (Princeton, N.J.: Princeton University Press, 1955), pp. 434–40.

10. See the article by Magnus Ottosson, *'erets*, in G. J. Botterweck and H. Ringgren, eds., *Theological Dictionary of the Old Testament*, vol. 1 (Grand Rapids, Mich.: Eerdmans, 1974), pp. 388–405, esp. pp. 397–99. The quote is on p. 398.

11. J. G. Plöger, *'adamah*, in Botterweck and Ringgren, p. 90 (emphasis mine).

5. THE QUINCEAÑERA

1. For an anthropological treatment of rites of passage, see Victor Turner, *The Forest of Symbols* (Ithaca, N.Y.: Cornell University Press, 1967); Victor and Edith Turner, *Image and Pilgrimage in Christian Culture: Anthropological Perspectives* (New York: Columbia, 1978); Anthony Wallace, *Culture and Personality* (New York: Random House, 1961); and the classic work by Arnold van Gennep, *Les Rites de Passage* (Paris, 1909). I am grateful to Sr. Nancy Wellmeier for the references to the works of Victor Turner and Anthony Wallace.

2. This means that "rooting" grounds religious ritual in social reality. Or as Peter Berger puts it, "For the individual, existing in a particular religious world implies existing in the particular social context within which that world can retain its plausibility," Peter Berger, *The Sacred Canopy* (New York: Doubleday Anchor, 1969), p. 46. The notion of plausibility for a religious ritual is crucial for a community's self-understanding. See Berger's treatment of legitimation throughout the work.

3. See a useful treatment of the relationship between woman and fertility, especially with regard to the earth in Mircea Eliade, *Patterns in Comparative Religion* (New York: Sheed and Ward, 1958), pp. 239–62. This correlation is emphasized in ritual within agricultural societies. Hispanics in the Southwest generally have ancestral roots, and therefore religious traditions, in agricultural society.

4. A perceptive treatment of the relationship between creation and chaos from a biblical-theological perspective is that by Bernhard W. Anderson, *Creation versus Chaos: The Reinterpretation of Mythical Symbolism in the Bible* (Philadelphia: Fortress Press, 1987). Walter Harrelson puts the issue rather succinctly when he talks about the role of worship vis-à-vis creation and chaos. "Worship, then, is of central importance for the life of man; the world itself lapses into chaos and decay if the proper acts of worship do not bring about its renewal." Walter Harrelson, *From Fertility Cult to Worship* (New York: Doubleday Anchor, 1970), p. 3.

5. See Eliade's discussion of this transcendent aspect of the rite of passage. Mircea Eliade, *The Sacred and the Profane: The Significance of Religious Myth, Sym-*

bolism, and Ritual within Life and Culture (New York: Harcourt, Brace & World, 1959), pp. 186–87.

6. Found in *Pequeño Ritual* (Guadalajara, Mexico, 1985), pp. 284–90. The ritual provides several excellent pastoral suggestions to enhance the meaning of the celebration.

7. Sister Angela Erevia, MCDP, *Quince Años: Celebrating a Tradition* (San Antonio, Tex.: Missionary Catechists of Divine Providence, 1985). A brief theologico-pastoral analysis was done by Rev. Juan Romero for the Los Angeles archdiocesan liturgy newsletter. "La Quinceañera," *Liturgical Life* (Los Angeles: Office of Liturgy, n.d.) 1:4, pp. 2–4.

8. See above chapter 3, "The Nature of Revelation."

9. Typical of the discussion is that found in Otto Kaiser, *Isaiah 1–12*, Old Testament Library (Philadelphia: Westminster, 1972), pp. 96–106, especially pp. 100–105.

10. These two contrasting theological traditions of God's presence will be treated in more detail in the next chapter.

11. Von Rad sees the most important consideration to be that of the "sign" in this passage. The principal sign is the name Immanuel, and is interpreted as weal for believers and woe for unbelievers. Gerhard von Rad, *Old Testament Theology*, vol. 2 (New York: Harper & Row, 1965), pp. 173–74.

12. See discussion of this dynamic of tradition and history in chapter 3.

13. The Gospel writers, in their attempt to understand the meaning of Jesus, often looked to the Hebrew Scriptures. The evangelist Matthew was writing to a Jewish audience and so wanted to present Jesus as a fulfillment of prophetic expectations. Thus he saw Jesus as the full embodiment of the Immanuel theme (Mt. 1:22–23), viz. as "God with us." In the famous prologue to his Gospel, the evangelist John continued this theme when he spoke of the "word who pitched his tent in our midst" (Jn. 1:14).

14. C. R. North writes a well-balanced article on the Immanuel issue, giving a summary and evaluation of the history of interpretation. C. R. North, "Immanuel," *Interpreter's Dictionary of the Bible*, vol. E–J (Nashville, Tenn.: Abingdon Press, 1962), pp. 685–88. Particularly provocative is his observation: "The possibility must be considered that a prophecy may have a proximate fulfillment which nevertheless does not exhaust its meaning," p. 688.

15. See the useful commentaries by Robert G. Boling and G. Ernest Wright, *Joshua*, Anchor Bible (Garden City, N.Y.: Doubleday & Co., 1982); and J. Alberto Soggin, *Joshua*, Old Testament Library (Philadelphia: Westminster, 1972).

16. See Boling and Wright, *Joshua*, p. 533.

17. For historical and archaeological study of this famous site see G. Ernest Wright, *Shechem: Biography of a Biblical City* (New York: McGraw-Hill, 1965).

18. The classic study on the Hittite suzerainty treaty pattern and the Old Testament is that by George E. Mendenhall, "Covenant Forms in Israelite Tradition," *Biblical Archaeologist* 17 (1954), pp. 50–76. Mendenhall describes Josh. 24 on pp. 67ff.

19. See discussion of this notion in Soggin, *Joshua*, pp. 236–39. For a more extensive and incisive treatment of the Sinai/Shechem question, see Delbert R. Hillers, *Covenant: The History of a Biblical Idea* (Baltimore: Johns Hopkins, 1970), pp. 46–71.

20. For an incisive treatment of the male/female aspects of Yahweh in the

TANAK, see Foster R. McCurley, *Ancient Myths and Biblical Faith* (Philadelphia: Fortress Press, 1983), esp. chapter 5, "The Nature of Yahweh and Human Sex." McCurley observes: "While God is neither male nor female, God is understood and described by humans in terms of the sexual roles of both sexes. God's role as creator of the world is communicated humanly speaking by roles assigned to male and female alike: to bear fruit and thus create human life throughout the earth," p. 99.

6. THE HOME ALTAR

1. Eliade, *The Sacred and the Profane*, p. 25.

2. G. van der Leeuw, *Religion in Essence and Manifestation*, vol. 2 (New York: Harper & Row, 1963), p. 397. Eliade speaks of the focal point as the "centre." See M. Eliade, *Images and Symbols* (New York: Sheed & Ward, 1961), pp. 39ff.; *Patterns in Comparative Religion* (New York: Sheed & Ward, 1958), pp. 379ff.

3. *Webster's New Universal Unabridged Dictionary* (New York: Simon & Schuster, 1979), p. 837.

4. Van der Leeuw, *Religion in Essence*, p. 398.

5. For a description of home altars in Texas, see Kay F. Turner, "Mexican-American Home Altars: Towards Their Interpretation," *Aztlan* 13:1–2 (1982), pp. 318–20. I find Turner's article interesting and informative, though I disagree with her central thesis that the Mexican-American home altar is a kind of women's folk art. It is, rather, a genuine faith-expression of religiosidad popular, which gives it greater complexity. For a solid discussion on the sociological and theological role of saints, which can be used in home altars, see Steele's treatment of saints in New Mexican iconography. Thomas J. Steele, *Santos and Saints: The Religious Folk Art of Hispanic New Mexico* (Santa Fe, N. Mex.: Ancient City Press, 1982).

6. For an excellent historical study of the relationship between the two, see the classic 1947 article by Frank M. Cross, "The Priestly Tabernacle," reprinted in *The Biblical Archaeologist Reader*, vol. 1, eds. G. Ernest Wright and David Noel Freedman (New York: Doubleday Anchor, 1961), pp. 201–28.

7. For example, the position of Frank Cross is fairly representative: " . . . the desert era was the creative and normative period of Israel's political and religious history, and this development was fomented and led by a revolutionary spirit, no doubt that of Moses." Cross, "The Priestly Tabernacle," p. 208.

8. The classic nineteenth-century study of Julius Wellhausen on the documentary hypothesis has since undergone major modification so that now scholars speak of traditions rather than documents in the Pentateuch. The most comprehensive study on the Pentateuchal sources is that by Martin Noth and Bernhard W. Anderson, *A History of Pentateuchal Traditions*, tr. B.W. Anderson (Missoula, Mont.: Scholar's Press Reproductions Series, 1981).

9. This seems to be the common scholarly opinion. The major articles discussing the relationship between the Tent and the Ark are those by Gerhard von Rad, "The Tent and the Ark," *The Problem of the Hexateuch and Other Essays* (New York: McGraw-Hill, 1966), pp. 103–24, and Roland de Vaux, "Ark of the Covenant and Tent of Reunion," *The Bible and the Ancient Near East* (New York: Doubleday, 1971), pp. 136–51. Two other useful articles are those by G. Henton Davies, "Ark of the Covenant," *Interpreter's Dictionary of the Bible*, vol. A–D (Nashville, Tenn.: Abingdon Press, 1962), pp. 222–26; and "Tabernacle," *Interpreter's Dictionary of the Bible*, vol. R–Z (Nashville, Tenn.: Abingdon Press, 1962), pp. 498–506. See also

R.E. Clements, *God and Temple* (Philadelphia: Fortress Press, 1965), esp. ch. 3, "The Ark, the Cherubim, and the Tent of Meeting," pp. 28–39.

10. As in the Greek New Testament equivalent of John 1:14, which speaks of the Logos "pitching his tent" *(eskenesen)* among us.

11. Cross, "The Priestly Tabernacle," pp. 226–27 (italics mine).

12. Von Rad connects the two in the Priestly document: ". . . initially the Tabernacle is to be regarded simply as a combination of Tent and Ark." Gerhard von Rad, *Old Testament Theology*, vol. 1 (London: Oliver & Boyd, 1963), p. 238.

13. For a detailed traditio-historical inquiry into the passage Ex. 33:7–11, see Walter Beyerlin, *Origins and History of the Oldest Sinaitic Traditions* (Oxford: Basil Blackwell, 1965), pp. 112–26. Beyerlin sees a cultic provenance for both shrines from earlier times. A more recent and exhaustive critical study of Ex. 33 is found in the commentary by Brevard Childs, *The Book of Exodus* (Philadelphia: Westminster Press, 1974), pp. 582–600. The priestly tradition of the Tabernacle/Tent is more concerned with its structuring, along the lines of the Jerusalem Temple. See Ex. 40:16-38 for example of P tradition.

14. Childs, *The Book of Exodus*, p. 590. See Cross, "The Priestly Tabernacle," and Davies, "Tabernacle," p. 505.

15. "The cloud is always linked to a manifestation of God. It signifies both presence and transcendence, it presupposes that God comes down to earth but that he is in heaven. This is why in Jewish and then Christian eschatology the cloud is the sign of heaven descending to earth or of a return to heaven. . . . The cloud, like the manna, ceased to exist when the Israelites reached the frontiers of the Promised Land." Yves Congar, *The Mystery of the Temple* (Westminster: Newman, 1962), pp. 9–10, 12. When the Israelites entered the promised land, the political system shifted from tribal federation to monarchy, so the struggle for making claim to divine presence – thus legitimating authority – came into full swing. See also Num. 11:24–25.

16. Walther Eichrodt, *Theology of the Old Testament*, vol. 1 (Philadelphia: Westminster Press, 1961), pp. 109–10.

17. As with the term "Lord of Hosts," *Yahweh-Sabaoth*, a distinctly military term.

18. Eichrodt, *Theology of the Old Testament*, pp. 230, 459.

19. An equally strong tradition of the Ark as reflecting Yahweh's presence among his people, leading them to victory, is found in the conquest story of Josh. 3–4. Chapter 3:10–11 is very explicit.

20. References in Jer. 7:12, 14 to this incident bear out the theory. See P. Kyle McCarter, *1 Samuel* (Garden City, N.Y.: Doubleday, The Anchor Bible, 1985), p. 109.

21. For a form-critical and traditio-historical study of the Ark narrative (I Sam. 4–6; II Sam. 6), see Antony F. Campbell, *The Ark Narrative*. SBL Dissertation Series 16 (Missoula, Mont.: Scholars Press, 1975).

22. Von Rad, "The Tent and the Ark," p. 118.

23. The Isaianic theme of Immanuel in Is. 7–12 and the Johannine doctrine of the Logos (Jn. 1:14) may well be offshoots of this theological stratum.

24. De Vaux argues that God's presence in the Ark was not so much permanent as it was a sometime thing. De Vaux, "Ark of the Covenant," pp. 147ff.

25. This is seen quite clearly in Jeremiah 5:12. The classic instance of a Davidic descendant eschewing responsibility for his actions is Jehoiakim in Jer. 22.

26. For an insightful commentary on the role of the Ark in 2 Sam. 6, see P. Kyle

McCarter, *II Samuel*. The Anchor Bible, vol. 9 (Garden City, N.Y.: Doubleday Anchor, 1984), esp. pp. 168–84; and for its connection with David's choice as king in 2 Sam. 7, cf. pp. 195–231.

27. This can be a concession to mediatorship, but it is also clear that the mediator is now part of the heavenly and not the earthly realm.

28. For further theological discussion of the home altar see C. Gilbert Romero, "Self-Affirmation of the Hispanic Church," *The Ecumenist* 23 (March–April 1985), pp. 39–42.

7. THE PENITENTES

1. Angelico Chavez, *My Penitente Land* (Albuquerque, N. Mex.: University of New Mexico, 1974).

2. Chavez, pp. 63–68. Quote is on p. 64.

3. Chavez, p. 65.

4. A good historical study of the Penitentes, complete with bibliography, is that by Marta Weigle, *Brothers of Light, Brothers of Blood* (Albuquerque, N. Mex.: University of New Mexico, 1976).

5. Thomas J. Steele and Rowena A. Rivera, *Penitente Self-Government* (Santa Fe, N. Mex.: Ancient City Press, 1985), pp. 5–6. This is an excellent work for understanding the early stages and inner workings of the brotherhood. Previously unavailable documents are presented.

6. These can be documented in some detail in the works cited by Weigle.

7. The relationship between the brotherhood and the official church is adequately covered in the works of Weigle and Steele/Rivera. Weigle is more thorough with regard to the origins of the brotherhood and church documentation regarding the brotherhood. See Weigle, *Brothers of Light*, pp. 19–51, and her conclusion: "In all likelihood, the problem of Penitente origins will never be decisively resolved," p. 49.

8. Because I was both a priest and a relative of some of the members, I was allowed to share in the rituals as much as a nonmember was permitted to do so. This experience is chronicled in my article, "Teología de las Raíces de un Pueblo: Los Penitentes de Nuevo Mexico," *Servir* 15 (1979), pp. 609–30.

9. The standard introductions to the Old Testament have sections on the wisdom literature. For a more comprehensive and insightful treatment of the wisdom material, see especially the works of Roland E. Murphy and James L. Crenshaw. For example, James L. Crenshaw, *Old Testament Wisdom: An Introduction* (Atlanta, Ga.: John Knox, 1981); *Studies in Ancient Israelite Wisdom* (New York: KTAV, 1976). Roland E. Murphy, *Seven Books of Wisdom* (Milwaukee, Wis.: Bruce, 1960); *Wisdom Literature: Job, Proverbs, Ruth, Canticle, Ecclesiastes, and Esther* (Grand Rapids, Mich.: Eerdmans, 1981); and the section "Introduction to Wisdom Literature," in *The New Jerome Biblical Commentary*, ed. R. Brown, J. Fitzmyer and R. Murphy (Englewood Cliffs, N.J.: Prentice-Hall, 1990), pp. 447–52; Roland Murphy, *The Tree of Life* (Garden City, N.Y.: Doubleday, The Anchor Bible, 1990).

10. James B. Pritchard, *Ancient Near Eastern Texts*, 2d ed. (Princeton, N.J.: Princeton University, 1955), pp. 405–407, 434–37.

11. For an interesting and incisive discussion of Yahweh as oppressive presence in Job, see James L. Crenshaw, *A Whirlpool of Torment: Israelite Traditions of God as an Oppressive Presence* (Philadelphia: Fortress Press, 1984), pp. 57–75.

12. Marvin H. Pope, *Job*, The Anchor Bible (New York: Doubleday & Co., 1965), p. lxxv.

13. Pope, p. lxxvi.

14. Pope, p. lxxviii.

15. Two useful commentaries on Qoheleth are those by James L. Crenshaw, *Ecclesiastes*, Old Testament Library. (Philadelphia: Westminster Press, 1987); and R.B.Y. Scott, *Proverbs. Ecclesiastes* (Garden City, N.Y.: Doubleday, The Anchor Bible, 1965).

16. Both the works by Weigle and Steele/Rivera describe the organizational structure of the brotherhood and explain in detail how this mutual help was provided.

17. Romero, *Servir*, pp. 626ff.

18. For further examples of this in the Penitente ritual, see Romero, *Servir*.

19. See footnotes 4 and 5.

8. CONCLUSIONS

1. See the argument in chapter 3 that discusses the relationship between foundational and dependent revelation with regard to religiosidad popular.

2. Justo L. Gonzalez, *Mañana: Christian Theology from a Hispanic Perspective* (Nashville, Tenn.: Abingdon Press, 1990).

3. Gonzalez, p. 72. For description of the Hispanic Protestant experience in the U.S., see pp. 66–73.

4. Gonzalez, p. 74.

5. Gonzalez offers some specifics of the danger of an "innocent reading" of history, pp. 78–80.

6. Gonzalez, p. 84.

7. Gonzalez, p. 85.

8. Ibid.

9. Ibid.

10. Gonzalez, p. 86.

11. Ibid.

12. Michael R. Candelaria, *Popular Religion and Liberation: The Dilemma of Liberation Theology* (Albany: SUNY Press, 1990). This work has an extensive bibliography that is helpful for further research into the topic of religiosidad popular.

13. Candelaria, p. xii. The citation in quotes is from Segundo Galilea.

14. Which is discussed in detail by Candelaria, pp. 39–67.

15. Also discussed in detail by Candelaria, pp. 69–101.

16. Candelaria, p. xiii.

17. Juan Luis Segundo's argument is more clearly developed in his *The Liberation of Theology* (Maryknoll, New York: Orbis Books, 1976), pp. 183–205 and pp. 208–37.

18. Juan Carlos Scannone, "Theology, Popular Culture, and Discernment," in *Frontiers of Theology in Latin America*, ed. Rosino Gibellini (New York: Orbis Books, 1979), pp. 213–39. The discussion in question is on pp. 221–22.

19. Scannone, pp. 223ff.

20. Candelaria, p. 66.

Index

'Ābad, 77

Academy of Catholic Hispanic Theologians, the, 3

Accompaniment, 120

'Ādām, 58, 65, 66

'Ādām-'adāmāh, 63, 64

'Adāmāh, 58, 65

Ad Gentes Divinitus (Vatican II), 39, 47-48, 120

'Āfār, 58, 65, 66

Ahaz, 74, 79

'Almāh, 75, 78, 79

Anthropology: Ash Wednesday and, 67-68; cultural, 24-27

Ark of the Covenant, the, 74, 88-89

Ashes: acceptance and, 68; biblical analogues of, 58-67; ceremony of, 66; doing justice and, 66; God's will and, 66; the limited good and, 67; reader-response criticism and, 67-68; redemptive quality of, 62-63; relationship with God and, 66-67; repentance and, 66; structuralism and, 67; as symbol of humbling attitude, 61; as symbol of mourning, 59-60; as symbol of penance, 60-61; as symbol of punishment, 58-59, 63; as symbol of suffering, 61-62

Ash Wednesday, 57-70: the Eucharist and, 57-58; explanation of, 57-58; insights from anthropology and hermeneutics, 67-68; pastoral implications of, 69-70; penitential dimension of, 57; revelatory aspect of, 68-69

Authority, centralization of in Church, 7

Babylonian Theodicy, the, 102

Baptismal promises, the Quinceañera and, 72-73

Barr, James, 43-44

Barragán, Javier Lozano, 32

Bible, the, devotional piety and, 15-33, 54-55

Bildad, 102, 103

Bishops, revelation and, 35, 37

Candelaria, Michael R., Popular Religion and Liberation: The Dilemma of Liberation Theology, 118

Casas, Bartolomé de las, 5

Castillo, Raul Duarte, 32

Catolicismo popular, 16

CELAM. See Puebla

Chavez, Angelico: on flagellation, 98-99; My Penitente Land, 98

Childs, Brevard, 87

"Christianity and Christendom," 5

Christianization: Enrique Dussel on, 6

Church, the: authority and, 7; Hispanics and, 5-14; the Penitentes and, 100; revelation and, 34-37

Closed corporate group, the, 24

Cloud, symbol of the, 87

Community service, the Quinceañera and, 72, 78

Conformity, liturgical, 7

Constitution on Divine Revelation (Vatican II). See Dei Verbum

Constitution on the Sacred Liturgy, the, 7

Covenant renewal ceremony, the, 76-78

Covenant traditions, Sinaitic and Davidic, 76

Cross, Frank, 86

"Cross and Crown," 5

Cultural anthropology, devotional piety and, 21-27

Culture, proper development of, 9-10

Davidic covenant model, the, 76, 91

Dei Verbum (Vatican II), 34-39

Deposit of faith, the, 37, 38

Devotional piety. *See* Piety, devotional

Diego, Juan, 49

Dulles, Avery: on cultural pluralism, 7; on revelation, 41-45, 46, 51

Dussel, Enrique, 6

Early Church, the, 17

Ecumenism, religiosidad popular and, 113-16

'Ēfer, 58, 59, 61, 65, 66

Egyptian Dispute Over Suicide, the, 102

Eichrodt, Walther, 87-89

Eliade, Mircea, 83

Eliphaz, 102, 103

'Erets, 59, 65

Erevia, Sr. Angela, 72

Eucharist, the, 57-58

Evangelii Nuntiandi (Paul VI), 8, 11, 16, 117

Evangelization: Medellín and, 10-11; popular religiosity and, 8-9

Faith, devotional piety and, 17-19

Fertility, the Quinceañera and, 71-72

Galilea, Segundo, 18-19

Gaudium et Spes (Vatican II), 9-10

God Who Acts: Biblical Theology as Recital (Wright), 43

Gonzalez, Justo L.: on ecumenism, 114; *Mañana: Christian Theology from a Hispanic Perspective*, 114; on "reading the Bible in Spanish," 115-16, 121

Guadalajara, Archdiocese of, 72

Guadalupe Hidalgo, Treaty of, 64

Guarani Indians, the, 6

Henan, Ernest, 18

Hermeneutics: Ash Wednesday and, 67-68; definition of, 36-37; devotional piety and, 27-32; historical-critical method, 27, 31, 37, 40; reader-response criticism, 30-32, 40; revelation and, 39; rhetorical criticism and, 28; structuralism, 28-30, 40

Hispanic Presence: Challenge and Commitment (U.S. Catholic Bishops), 14

Hispanics: and the Church, 5-14; heterogeneity of, 15-16

Historical-critical method, the, 27, 31, 37, 39

History, revelation and, 43-44, 50-51

Hittite suzerainty treaty pattern, the, 77

Home altar, the, 83-97: analogues to, 85-89, 91-94; the Ark of the Covenant and, 88-89; the Church and, 84; explanation of, 83-84; pastoral implications of, 96-97; perception of limited good and, 92; reader-response criticism and, 93; revelatory aspect of, 94-96; structuralism and, 93; the Tent of Meeting and, 85-88

Humbling attitude, ashes and, 61

Imagery, religious, 32

Immanence, theology of, 90-91, 92, 93

Immanuel, sign of, 74, 75, 79

Individual, the, 24, 26

Instituto de Liturgia Hispana, the, 3

Instituto Superior de Pastoral, the, 2

Job, 101-104

Justice, doing, 66

Keegan, Terence J.: on mythic structures, 29-30; on reader-response criticism, 31; on structuralism, 28, 29

Kinship and marriage, 25-27

Knight, Douglas, 42-43

Kraft, Charles, 21-22

La Hermandad de Nuestro Padre Jesus Nazareno, 98

Land, Hispanic connection with, 64-66

Language: devotional, 7; symbolism and, 52-53

Latin American Bishops' Conference. *See* Medellín

Lemke, Werner, 44

Liberation: Puebla on, 116-17, 121; religiosidad popular and, 116-19

Liberation theology, Medellín and, 10

Limited good, the, perception of, 67, 92

Literature: apocalyptic, 61; wisdom, 61, 101, 104

Ludlul Bel Nemeqi, 102

Macquarrie, John, 38
Maher-shalal-hash-baz, 74
Maldonado, Fr. Luis, 2, 7
Malina, Bruce: on kinship, 25-26; on models of cultural anthropology, 24-27; *The New Testament World: Insights from Cultural Anthropology,* 23
Mañana: Christian Theology from a Hispanic Perspective (Gonzalez), 114
Medellín, 10-13; *Pastoral Popular,* 16
The Mission, 5-6
Mordechai, 59
Mourning, ashes as symbol of, 59-60, 63
My Penitente Land (Chavez), 98
Myth: devotional piety and, 18; structures of, 29-30
Narrative, deep structures of, 29
National Plan for Hispanic Ministry (U.S. Catholic Bishops), 14
The New Testament World: Insights from Cultural Anthropology (Malina), 23
O'Collins, Gerald, 38-39
Old Testament, the, 20
Oñate, Juan de, 1, 98, 99
On the Move (Sandoval), 3
'*Oth,* 74
Otto, Rudolf, 17
Our Lady of Guadalupe, 49, 50-51
Pannenberg, Wolfhart, *Revelation as History,* 43
Pastoral Popular (Medellín), 10, 16
Paul VI, *Evangelii Nuntiandi,* 8, 11, 16, 117
Pe'ēr, 59
Penance, ashes as symbol of, 60-61, 63-64
Penitentes, the, 40, 98-112: analogues to, 101-109; the Church and, 100; explanation of, 98-101; pastoral implications of, 111-12; revelatory aspect of, 109-11
Perception of the limited good, 24-27
Piedad popular, 16
Piety, popular: the Bible and, 15-33; cultural anthropology and, 21-27; definition of, 11-12; Ernest Henan on, 18; faith and, 17-19; Herman

Vorlander on, 20; hermeneutical theory and, 27-32; Javier Lozano Barragán on, 32; Medellín and, 11; myth and, 18; negative aspects of, 13; the Old Testament and, 20; Puebla on, 16; Raul Vidales on, 20; revelation and, 34-56; Segundo Galilea on, 18-19; values of, 12-13
Plöger, J. G., 66
Pluralism, cultural, 7
Pope, Marvin, 103, 104
Popular Religion and Liberation: The Dilemma of Liberation Theology (Candelaria), 118
Puebla: dependent revelation and, 40; evangelization and, 11-13; liberation and, 116-17, 121; popular piety and, 16
Punishment, ashes as symbol of, 58-59, 63
Qoheleth, challenges of, 104-107
Quinceañera, the, 71-82: analogues to, 73-80; baptismal promises and, 72-73; community service and, 72; explanation of, 71 73; fertility and, 71-72; pastoral implications of, 81-82; reader-response criticism and, 79; revelatory aspect of, 80-81; right order and, 72; structuralism and, 79
Rad, Gerhard Von, 90
Reader-response criticism, 30-32, 116: ashes and, 67-68; the home altar and, 93; postulates of, 79; the Quinceañera and, 79; revelation and, 39
"Reading the Bible in Spanish," 115-16
Relationship with God, ashes and, 66-67
Relativism, cultural, 21-22
Religiosidad popular: the Bible and, 54-55; ecumenism and, 113-16; evangelization and, 8-9; liberation and, 116-19; pastoral orientation, 119-21; revelation and, 34-56. *See also* Piety, devotional
Re-memorization, 120-21
Repentance, ashes and, 66
Retribution principle, the, 102, 103, 104, 105, 107
Revelation: Avery Dulles on, 41-45, 46;

Church teaching on, 34 37; definition of, 36; dependent, 39, 40, 45; foundational, 38, 39, 46; function of, 45-47; Gerald O'Collins on, 38-39; historical-critical method and, 39; history and, 43-44, 50-51; human experience and, 61; John Macquarrie on, 38; nature of, 41-45; Paul Ricoeur on, 46-47; Paul Tillich on, 38; reader-response criticism and, 39; religiosidad popular and, 34-56; structuralism and, 39; symbol and, 45, 51-53; tradition and, 42-43, 48-53; Werner Lemke on, 44

Revelation as History (Pannenberg), 43

Rhetorical criticism, 28

Ricoeur, Paul, 46-47

Right order, the Quinceañera and, 72

Rivera, Rowena, 99-100

Roman Catholic Church. *See* Church, the

Romero, Fr. Juan, 3

Sacraments, function of, 32

Sacrosanctum Concilium (Vatican II), 8

St. Anthony of Padua, 84

St. Jude, 84

Sandoval, Moises, *On the Move*, 3

Satirical Letter of Hori, the, 102

Scannone, Juan Carlos, 118-19

Scripture, revelation and, 35, 37

Second Vatican Council. *See* Vatican II

Segundo, Juan Luis, 118

Self-assertion, devotional piety as, 17

Self-flagellation, 98

Shear-Yashub, 74

Shechem, 76

Sinai covenant, the, 76, 77, 87, 91, 93, 94

Song of the Ark, the, 88

Sophar, 102, 103

Stations of the Cross, the, 110

Steele, Thomas, 99-100

Structuralism, 116: ashes and, 67; the

home altar and, 93; the Quinceañera and, 79; revelation and, 39

Suffering: ashes as symbol of, 61-62; of the innocent, 101-104

Supracultural, concept of, 21, 26

Symbol, revelation and, 45, 51-53

Symbolism: Avery Dulles on, 51; in devotional practice, 51-52; through language, 52-53

Symbolization, model of, 26

Tamar, 59

Tent and Ark theologies, political implications of, 89-91

Tent of Meeting, the, 74, 85-88

Tepeyac, Mount, 49

Tercer Encuentro Nacional Hispano de Pastoral, 14

"Third Orders," 98

Tillich, Paul, 38

Tradition: definition of, 36; revelation and, 35, 37, 42-43, 48-53

Transcendence, theology of, 91

U.S. Catholic Bishops: *Hispanic Presence: Challenge and Commitment*, 14; *National Plan for Hispanic Ministry*, 14

Validvieso, Antonio, 5

van der Leeuw, Gerhardus, 83, 84

Vatican II: *Ad Gentes Divinitus*, 47-48; Constitution on the Sacred Liturgy, 7; *Dei Verbum*, 34-37; *Gaudium et Spes*, 9-10; *Sacrosanctum Concilium*, 8

Vergegenwärtigung, 43, 73

Veronica, 110

Vidales, Raul, 20, 32

Vorländer, Herman, 20

Wisdom movement, Hebrew, 105

Wright, G. Ernest, *God Who Acts: Biblical Theology as Recital*, 43

Yahweh, as warrior-god, 88, 89, 93-94, 95, 96

"Young woman," the, 74-76

Zubiría, Bishop, 100